CITY OF WRONG
A Friday in Jerusalem

――――― ❖ ―――――

About the translator

Kenneth Cragg is a distinguished scholar of Islamic and Christian Studies. His many books on the Qur'án and Arab Christianity, including *The Event of the Qur'án* (also published by Oneworld) have become classics in their field. During his time in Cairo as Study Secretary of the Near East Christian Council and as Anglican Bishop, he formed a close friendship with Dr Kamel Hussein (d. 1977), at whose request he translated this work, *Qaryah Zálimah*, into English. Bishop Cragg obtained his doctorate at Oxford University, and has served in academic and ecclesiastical posts in Jerusalem, Beirut, Cairo, Nigeria and the USA. In retirement he serves as an Honorary Assistant Bishop in the Diocese of Oxford.

Mystical Classics of the World Series

Evelyn Underhill. *Mysticism: The Nature and Development of Spiritual Consciousness*

Evelyn Underhill. *The Spiritual Life: Great Spiritual Truths for Everyday Life*

Kahlil Gibran. *Jesus the Son of Man*

Brother Lawrence. *The Practice of the Presence of God*

R.C. Zaehner. *Hindu & Muslim Mysticism*

Edwin A. Abbott. *Flatland: A Parable of Spiritual Dimensions*

W. Montgomery Watt. *The Faith & Practice of Al-Ghazálí*

Margaret Smith. *Rábi'a: The Life & Work of Rábi'a and other Women Mystics in Islam*

# City of Wrong

## A Friday in Jerusalem

M. Kamel Hussein

Translated from the Arabic with an Introduction by
Kenneth Cragg

ONEWORLD
OXFORD

CITY OF WRONG

Oneworld Publications
(Sales and Editorial)
185 Banbury Road
Oxford OX2 7AR
England

Oneworld Publications
(U.S. Sales Office)
42 Broadway
Rockport, MA 01966
USA

© Kenneth Cragg 1994

All rights reserved.
Copyright under Berne Convention
A CIP record for this book is available
from the British Library

ISBN 1-85168-072-1

Printed and bound in Finland by WSOY

## Contents

Preface 7
**1. Introduction** 9
*Ecce Homines* 11

**2. Friday** 27

**3. In Jewry** 31
*The Mountain Top* 33
*The Prosecutor* 35
*A Blacksmith's Shop* 41
*The Mufti* 51
*Lazarus* 57
*Caiaphas* 65
*The Hall of Meeting* 78

**4. With the Disciples** 89
*Woman of Magdal* 91
*The Christian Soldier* 104
*A Sick Girl* 110
*The Disciples in Conference* 118
*The Disciples' Departure* 137

**5. Among the Romans** 147
*A Resolute Commander* 149
*The Traitor* 153
*Trial and Sentence* 169
*Pilate* 180

**6. Golgotha and After**   187
*Darkness Over All the Land*   189
*Return to the Sermon on the Mount*   202
*Conclusion*   214

**Annexes**   219
*Translator's Footnotes*   221
*Author's Note: The Apostles' Self-Reproach*   232

# Preface

Written in Arabic in the early fifties and translated in the late fifties, Muhammad Kamel Hussein's *Qaryah Zálimah*, or *City of Wrong*, with three editions in the sixties, has been too long out-of-print. The Introduction, *Ecce Homines*, written in Jerusalem thirty-six years ago, still sufficiently sets out its remarkable significance. It is good that this should be accessible to a whole new generation in inter-faith studies and Muslim–Christian relationships around the salient shared themes of a partly mutual theism and the questions about God, Christ, the Scriptures and the human predicament that remain at issue.

In his deep humanism and urgent interest in peace, Dr Hussein sensed a vital arena for his thought and care in the habit of 'collectives', whether of nation, party, race or dogma, to absolutise their claims and override the otherwise restraining factor of personal conscience. He identified a dramatic example of this false absolutising of power and corporate vested-interest in the will to crucify Jesus. Leaving aside the issues about a theology of the Cross and, with it, also the painful controversies about what could, or could not, be predicated about God in terms of redemptive, suffering love, he concentrated on that 'will to crucify' as an index to how wrong humanity could be. Thus he focused in the very core of Christian history and faith the question of sinful expediency. We differ about its diagnosis and the cost of its correction, and how our differing convictions about either might relate. It is because they are so crucial to the nations and their peace, as well as to God and His credentials, that it is well to have again in print, for a yet more urgent time, the imaginative narrative skill, the warm, incisive wisdom, and the disciplined mind of a notable son of Cairo and witness from Jerusalem. His friendship is among the warmest experiences I had in both capitals.

KENNETH CRAGG
*Oxford, 1994*

# 1. Introduction

# Ecce Homines

Readers of the Gospels have often been uneasily aware that in their verdict against Jesus men were in fact involved in an inclusive verdict against themselves. The Governor Pilate's familiar cry, in presenting the Prisoner to the pity and, as it finally proved, to the brutality of the mob with the words: *Ecce Homo*, 'Behold the Man,' turns on reflection into the plural. Here more than anywhere humankind is discernible in representative moral perversity, epitomised in ecclesiastical, political and popular choices made by particular people caught in a personal and communal crisis. The *Ecce Homo* scene in the precincts of the Roman praetorium presents a man to the judgement of a crowd. But such are its implications that the tables are reversed. The man becomes the crisis of the crowd and the moral meaning of the scene becomes a judgement by and of humanity. All its import gathers into one revelation chief priests and people, governor and onlookers, and cries to us all: *Ecce Homines*, 'Behold humanity.'

The fascination of this book is that this theme has here been sensitively explored and presented, probably for the first time, by a thinker from within the faith of Islam. For the first time, inasmuch as the great and vast household of Islam down the centuries has been adamantly disposed to deny the crucifixion of Jesus of Nazareth. Where Christians ever since the first Muslim century have been at pains to re-assert the event, the upshot, for the most part, has been a strife about historicity which, important as it was, and remains, has tended to obscure the significance in and beyond the history. The author of the book here offered to English readers invites his fellow Muslims to transcend the resultant polemic and, without transgressing the Quranic limits on which the Muslim belief that the crucifying of Jesus did not happen depends, makes a penetrating analysis of the will to His crucifixion.

It may be well at the outset to clarify briefly the sum of what the Qur'án, the holy Book of Islam, has to say on the Cross of Christ. The pivotal passage is that in Surah iv. 156, which reads: 'They (i.e. the Jews) say: We killed the Messiah, 'Isá, (Quranic name for Jesus), son of Mary, the apostle of God. But they did not kill him, nor did they crucify him. It seemed so to them. Those who had altercations on this matter are dubious about it, and in fact in the absence of sound knowledge are following conjectures. The sure fact is they did not kill him. On the contrary, God raised him to Himself, God the strong and the wise.' The context of controversy and dispute here referred to may reflect certain docetic tendencies in early heretical Christianity which, for various mainly metaphysical reasons, questioned the possibility of the Messiah being literally and actually a sufferer. The attitudes of Islam reproduce many of these misgivings and may derive from them historically. But the main immediate point is the exegesis of the denial in its Quranic form. The prevailing view is that at some point, undetermined, in the course of the final events of Christ's arrest, trial and sentence, a substitute person replaced Him while Jesus Himself was, in the phrase, raised or raptured into Heaven, from whence, unscathed and uncrucified, He returned to His disciples in personal appearances in which He commissioned them to take His teachings out into the world. The Gospel they were thus to preach was a moral law only and not the good tidings of a victorious, redemptive encounter with sin and death. Meanwhile, the substitute sufferer bore the whole brunt of the historical crucifixion, having been sentenced and condemned *as if he were the Christ*.

It is this important phrase on which the whole possibility of *City of Wrong* turns as a Muslim study of Christ crucified. The Quranic text is somewhat enigmatic, since in Arabic the 'hidden' pronoun in the passive verb, translated 'made to seem so' may refer to crucifixion ('it') or to Jesus ('He'). In the first case, the meaning would be that death by crucifixion 'seemed to happen' but in fact did not. The victim was Jesus in person and He was Himself actually and physically nailed to the Cross. But He did not there succumb. When taken down from the instrument of death, He had not in fact expired. Subsequently, in the tomb, He revived and was 'spirited away' (quite physically if the phrase may be permitted) by the disciples. Other Quranic references to His death (as in Surah iii. 56, iv. 158 and ix. 33) relate to His ultimate demise, after, in some authorities, His long, teaching sojourn in Asia. This version, held in the last century by members of the Ahmadiyyah sects of Islam, is entirely unacceptable in orthodox circles.

There the pronoun in question is taken as personal and relating to Jesus. It means that He was not killed nor crucified, not in the sense that He did not succumb and die by crucifixion, but that He never came into the position of a victim. The 'seeming' was not a 'death' (only apparent) on *His* part, but a mistake in identity, seemingly ordered and arranged by God's intervention, on account of which another victim, having all the personal appearance of Jesus, was by error condemned and executed *as if he had been Him*. References to Christ's death elsewhere in the Qur'án, on this view, concern His ultimate, post-millennial demise and burial in Medina beside the Prophet of Islam.

But in either case – and overwhelmingly so on this second and prevailing orthodox exegesis – the human antecedents of the Cross are exactly what they are in the Christian understanding. If we shelve, for the moment, the question whether the Cross happened to Jesus and concentrate on the event as something which was intended for Jesus, the whole of the human significance of the decision against Him and for His death, as taken by His contemporaries, remains unimpaired. It is upon this that Dr. Muhammad Kamel Hussein fixes and Muslim comment on his work takes careful cognisance of this point. The author remains strictly within his Quranic grounds. The interesting thing is that few, if any, before him have taken a specifically Muslim initiative to study the Christian history on its human side.

One clear result of his work is to remind Christians that they should think again before they crudely and hastily assert that the Muslim holy Book denies the Cross. In a very crucial sense it affirms it. For the Cross is not only a redemptive deed which Christ embraces as both messianically and Divinely central to love's scheme for human retrieval and forgiveness. It is also, seen from the human side, the deed of rejection in which the perpetrators registered their verdict against the teaching and personality of Jesus. The crucifiers were not dastardly criminals thirsting for anybody and everybody's blood (the violent men were then themselves on crosses with Jesus). They were representatives of a highly meticulous and lofty religion, who, for their own communal reasons, wanted a particular teacher silenced and put out of the way. Before they could accomplish their end, the wrongly identified victim (on the Muslim showing) had to be given all the physical and human features of the one Jesus, before they would do him, erroneously, to death. Clearly neither Caiaphas, nor Pilate, nor the crowd, were crucifying a substitute *qua* substitute. Had they known the mistake in identity they would have desisted at once. Had that not been the case, no Divine occasion of their deception would have been necessary. It is unmistakeably clear, through all the tortuous controversy over 'made to seem so to them,' that the Qur'án affirms incontrovertibly that, at least as far as the intention of the perpetrators was concerned, the Cross on Golgotha was the Cross of Jesus. All the antecedent antipathy which reached its climax in this decision for His death constituted, with that death (considered as men's intention), a tremendous moral encounter in which the issues of the human situation are mirrored and the inclusive crisis of humanity can be studied. It is this the author has set himself to understand and depict. The fact that he does so from within a system of faith and practice which traditionally neglects the implications of its own sacred, scriptural affirmation of Christ as a Teacher people so desperately willed to refuse that to thwart them required a Divine *ex machina* rescue of this sort involving *His* crucifixion by proxy, is what gives to *City of Wrong* its uniqueness and force. Whether or not the question about Who was central in the Cross as a culmination, as distinct from who was central in the Cross as a growing encounter of decision, can be rightly ignored will concern us at the end of this Introduction.

The author of *City of Wrong* has had a distinguished career as a surgeon and an educationalist, whose interests have taken him into literature and philosophy as well as into the obscurer reaches of his own professional field. Thus he has written on ancient Egyptian medicine, including a translation of an old treatise from hieroglyphics, and on early Arab medical science, with special reference to fractures of the skull. He is a former President of Ibrahim 'Ain al-Shams University in Cairo. Problems of Quranic interpretation, both scientific and moral, have also engaged his attention and one of his most penetrating ventures in this field was a paper on *Zulm* in the Qur'án – a term whose import bears considerably on the theme of the present book and which will be discussed below. Of his published work in the realm of literary criticism and essays, mention may be made of *Mutanawwi'át* (Miscellany) which contains a discussion on the Arabic eloquence of the Qur'án, a study of the Islamic poet Al-Mutanabbi, excursions into ancient science and an intriguing comparison between Christology in Christian thought and Muslim theological debates on the uncreated status of the Qur'án. He has also given evidence of a close interest in the significance of Jewish history and has written on the meaning of the Exodus and Biblical ethics.

He thus brings to the immediate study of the events of Good Friday a wide familiarity with religious thought and an incisive, sensitive mind. What, the reader may ask, is the main theme of *Qaryah Zálimah*, to use the Arabic title of *City of Wrong*? It is occupied with the appeal beyond conscience to the collective in human affairs, the wrong of our slavishness to communal interest and the inability of religion or law to save us from our tragic rebellion against the truth of conscience unless they themselves, that is, religion and law, are properly related to truth in the capacity of servants not masters. These are the deep topics of the present work, with reflections on the alleged pre-occupation of Christianity with sin, and upon the urgency of the call for the repudiation of war, and of political tyranny in the support of religious values. The concept of all things under God, which, in the author's view, means all things under conscience, lies at the very heart of the concept of *Islam*, by which all things are right only when they are rightly related to the lordship of God.

It is in the circumstances of the Friday when the world, epitomised in Jerusalem under Caiaphas and Pilate, was in the throes of its moral encounter with truth and right, embodied in Jesus of Nazareth, that the writer finds the central occasion and the essential core of his theme. It may be illustrated by a somewhat extended quotation from Martin Buber's *Between Man and Man* where the same disquiet about the collective as our all too frequent plea to justify wrong is movingly expressed. The topic in Buber is the suspension of the Ten Commandments in the Palestine of 1948. Could murder ever become a good deed in the name of one's group? Are we to assume that the veto against false witness carries the proviso: 'Whenever it does not profit you'? One of the interlocutors replies:

'"But it is not a question of my profit, but the profit of my people. There all question of 'I' disappears."

'Teacher: "Then if you are thinking: We want victory, don't you feel at the same time: I want victory?"

'Pupil: "But the people, that is something infinitely more than just the people of today. It includes all past and future generations." At this point the teacher felt the moment had come to leave the narrow compass of the present and to invoke historical destiny. He said: "Yes! all past generations. But what was it that made those past generations of the Exile live? What made them live and overcome all their trials? Wasn't it that the cry 'Thou shalt not' never faded from their hearts and ears?"

The pupil grew very pale. He was silent for a while, but it was the silence of one whose words threatened to stifle him. Then he burst out: "And what have we achieved that way . . . . ?"'[1]

Here, essentially, in another context, is the theme of *City of Wrong*: a people or their representatives exonerating themselves by an appeal to the interests of a community extended in time, whose collective will becomes itself an absolute, overriding even the moral obligations inherent in its own heritage. The phrase *Qaryah*

Zálimah occurs in Surahs xxi. 11 and xxii. 44 and 47 of the Qur'án. Qaryah is strictly a village or township but since it refers here to Jerusalem 'city' becomes the only possible translation. Zálimah is the active participle from the root Zalama, giving the verbal noun Zulm, already mentioned. It is a root which occurs some 150 or more times in the Qur'án in various forms, and means essentially to act wrongfully, unjustly or tyrannically, or when transitive to wrong or treat injuriously. Zulm is the act of deviating from what is proper in one's treatment of things, people, property, trust. There is a Zulm between a person and God, between one person and another and between a person and himself or herself. Each finds frequent mention in Quranic settings, not least the last in the oft asserted truth about sinners: 'It was their own selves they wronged.' Zulm is something of which God is never guilty. 'He does not despoil them of the weight of one of the smallest of ants.' (Surah iv. 44) But it is our besetting evil, the sin of *hybris*, the wrong of false absolutes to which we bring our distorted and destroying allegiances, doing despite to our true vocation and our proper role. The whole concept is wide, inclusive and tremendous and involves sins political, religious, social and personal, inasmuch as there is no arena of our conduct and being exempt from the reach of our chronic perversity.

Jerusalem, then, is a representative locus of the representative wrongness of the world, when, on Black Friday, it wrongs Jesus, and in Him, God, Jerusalem and humanity, in the act which elects that He be crucified. But it is a *City of Wrong* which symbolises humanity at large. It is a community of wrongdoing not as being Jerusalemite, or Jewish, Palestinian or Roman, but as being human. Qaryah Zálimah is not an indictment of a race but of a deed, not of a community in itself but of a community in its action. No reader need suppose that here is some kind of subtle reproach of Jewry masquerading as a lament over the crucifixion, such as has been known at times in the west. Indeed it is just the depth of implicit Muslim self-criticism within the themes of this work, which makes Dr. Muhammad Kamel Hussein so moving and eloquent a writer.

For the extent to which he deliberately expresses attitudes he deplores, in specifically Islamic terms, makes his work so clear a warning to Muslims as well as those outside Islam. Thus the prosecutor here expatiates to the merchant on the sacredness of the law in the very phrase with which Surah ii. 2 and numerous other passages commend the Qur'án 'a book, indubitable'. Yet the attitude of such obedience is plainly and properly in the pillory. The mufti, likewise, with the obvious approval of the author, complains that the vulgar throng follow anyone who will make (false) claims to certitude, lest they have to think and criticise. Again, the very phrase used is the Qur'án's own, commending its indubiety (p. 56). Similarly the familiar Islamic concept of *Ijmá'*, or consensus, is pleaded by persons in the wrong, to justify on grounds of collective necessity the decisions by which they flout the right. 'Not agreeing on an error' (the idea which lies at the heart of the Islamic appeal to the safety of numbers, the validity of what the whole approves, heresy being misguided individualism, and orthodoxy that which the collective whole adopts) is used at the very point where the mob rushes into the hall of assembly and brusquely cuts short any private misgivings that falter and hesitate about the popular verdict against Jesus. It is hardly a context which does credit to the principle (p. 85).

The involvement of Islam in the themes of *City of Wrong* is both essentially and verbally clear in many other places. The prosecutor calls upon the assembly to 'cut off this disruptive evil,' referring to the message and influence of the Galilean prophet (p. 52). The word used is *Fitnah*, a Quranic expression of considerable complexity. In some senses it means merely 'trial' or 'test of loyalty' as when, for example, the early Muslim fighters found the wish to stay safely with their children and evade battle duty a 'temptation' (*Fitnah*) (Surah viii. 28). But in other more frequent contexts the word has the implication of sedition and civil strife which jeopardise the political progress of Islam. Such *Fitnah* is to be forcibly countered until it surrenders. This selfsame plea of *Fitnah*, the enormity to be smashed and broken, is used against Jesus, by pleaders like the prosecutor who are nevertheless plainly in the wrong. In other words the attitudes by which early Islam subdued and broke the gainsayers are reproduced here in the campaign against Jesus by the Jews who were His contemporaries. No doubt this theme of Jewish perversity in their treatment of the prophets has broad Quranic sanction. But it is startling to find them thus associated with what, vis-à-vis the idolaters in Mecca, was traditionally considered a highly commendable attitude befitting Islam. The implications are worked out in the later philosophical passages on the futility and repudiation of violence and force in religious service. The disciples too, discuss saving Jesus, obviously misguidedly, in the same general terms. Perhaps most significant of all is the far-reaching and eloquent interpretation the author gives to the characteristic Islamic concept of *Shirk*, the cardinal sin. The term means, essentially, the evil of *Zulm* against God, where God is improperly regarded or disregarded, where He is accorded less than or other than His proper place in men's worship, obedience and surrender. The commonest forms, in the first days of Islam, of such *Shirk* were those arising, of course, from idolatry. For to substitute an idol for God is manifestly to do Him wrong and despite. Idolatry has almost entirely monopolised ever since the Muslim idea of what *Shirk* is, partly perhaps because it is relatively easy to castigate polytheists when one is in no danger of being one, or to shatter with an eager iconoclasm the 'gods' that are amenable to destruction by hammers. But it is clear to Dr. Hussein and to anyone with the imagination to follow his thought that idolatry is very far from being the only serious form of *Shirk*. Any loyalty that displaces God by claiming a false absolutism of its own is *Shirk*. And many of these take more than iconoclastic hammers to dispose of. There are idols of trade and race and nation and creed. It is possible even for Islam in certain manifestations to displace in people's loyalty the very God to whom it witnesses, if it becomes thereby an end in and unto itself. Similarly, nationalism undisciplined to the larger human whole, or economic systems that claim false autonomy, preaching that what is good for them is good, are idolatries. In pioneering within Islam a deep present-day relevance in the Islamic anathema on *Shirk*, the author of *City of Wrong* has opened wide vistas of thought and action.

Other aspects of the book's penetrating honesty about the temptations of religion, including Islam and Christianity, will be clear from the footnotes. The instinct throughout is honesty in human diagnosis with no reservations and immunities. If for a day of our times we substitute a far-away day in A.D. 28, we might well borrow the words of a poem of Walter de la Mare:

> *Engrossed in the day's 'news', I read*
> *Of all in men that's vile and base;*
> *Horrors confounding heart and head –*
> *Massacre, murder, filth, disgrace:*
> *Then paused. And thought did inward tend –*
> *On my own past, and self, to dwell.*
> *Whereat some inmate muttered, 'Friend,*
> *If you and I plain truth must tell,*
> *Everything human we comprehend,*
> *Only too well, too well!'* [2]

It is just this affinity with our compromises and collective wrongs that brings that distant Friday contemporaneously near and makes the author's witness to us so deep an exercise in spiritual meeting across religious frontiers. So rare are such overtures from within Islam (though their rarity may be laid in part at the door of Christian non-expectancy) that persons of heart in the Christian world must lay hold of this one with both hands and an eager soul.

The Christian reader will probably find one central mystery, which the author has only partially clarified in the Appendix. He insists that the besetting mood of Christianity is one of self-reproach and an excessive pre-occupation with the sense of sin. This he links with the crisis of Good Friday and with the failure of the disciples physically to rescue Jesus from His foes. The puzzle lies in the fact that such rescue would have countered every aspect of Christ's teaching and purpose. How then could refraining from it have been sinful? Nor does it seem from a careful study of the text that the wrong lies in having blunderingly willed to effect such a rescue. On some counts such intended, though not executed, disloyalty to lessons taught might be held wrongful. But it does not appear that this is what the author has in mind. It is hard to see how it can be thought that failure to resist effectively despite Jesus' veto on all such action was the sin behind such perpetual reproach. The point remains puzzling. Nor is it eased by the suggestion that their sense of sin arose from their being disallowed to save Him. For that decision on Jesus' part came, not from any incompetence in them, but from deliberate principles of His Messiahship.

To the Christian within the faith it rather seems that the Christian sense of the sinfulness of sin derives precisely from that instinct to distrust all goods which the author so pointedly depicts. Even meticulous religion grievously strays. Empires proud of law and discipline commit the most fearful crimes. 'They would not enter the judgement hall lest they should be defiled' says the Gospel, of the chief priests (S. John xviii. 28). Yet they sensed nothing defiling in the will to make away with Christ. This strange mingling of legal scruple and utter moral blindness is a terrifying measure of the failure of all law and ideology. This sort of thing is the worst one can say about this world and our humanity – that it is the kind of place where these things can be. Christianity regards the Cross as the place, quite manifestly, of 'the sin of the world' not in quantitative accumulation, but in qualitative nature and disclosure. Is not this why redemption, regeneration, the remaking of our souls, become so urgent and so large a need?

For there is no end, otherwise, to this entail of wrongness. About all natural goodness there is an endlessly regressive evil character – the humility that is proud; the rightness that is unlovely; the meticulousness over law that is hard, censorious and vain; the capacity of people and communities to deceive themselves into chronic evil, foul and horrid, in the name of principle that is good and worthy. These are the human realities mirrored in the crucifying of Jesus. Because they are as they are, our only salvation lies in an inward making new of our souls, the condition of which is a perpetual penitence and a genuine humility. Could it be these, not asceticism, not brooding, not morbidity, which explain the characteristic Christian sense of undoneness and a proper concern to be liberated from the *Qaryah Zálimah* within the heart of every person? These considerations too might give pause about the adequacy of the book's solutions, as long as they remain mainly sermonic, or rely excessively on the realm of conscience. For there are times and occasions of deepest wrong where the essence of our astrayness is not the flouting of conscience, but its obedience, not the stifling of our inward protests, but the pursuit of their behests. Conscience remains a smoking flax, not, in truth to be quenched, but surely not to be relied upon for the wholeness of our salvation, involved and implicated as it is in the measure of our perversity.

These thoughts would also lie behind any Christian assessment of the Wise Man who does appear a little overpompous and hortatory in certain of these settings. It is hardly appropriate to indulge in merely philosophical abstractions at the foot of the Cross, however well-intentioned they may be. Nor is the essence of the sequel to the 'crucifixion' merely didactic. Indeed, considered as a persuasive teaching alone, the Gospel of Jesus meets its nadir at the Cross and is therein to all appearance bankrupt of achievement. It is victoriously proclaimed beyond the Cross because it is therein vested in a larger whole, in the drama of Divine Love through suffering both exemplifying and establishing it in an active principle of human transformation of which the Cross, suffered by the Saviour and acknowledged by the sinner, is the heart and core and nerve.

These thoughts are not offered here critically but reflectively, as part of that inter-religious community of thought and yearning which the author intends and which this translation is undertaken to serve. They lead to one final, but inclusive, consideration. Readers will notice that the central Figure in all these events is strangely absent from the centre of the scene. There may be valid artistic and perhaps spiritual reasons for that fact. Be these as they may, Jesus does not appear in person in the book, save briefly in the narrative of the conversion of Mary Magdalene. He is one to whom the disciples send for advice (though at that juncture they had no other option). The Sermon on the Mount is reported by the Wise Man and others. We do not hear it *in situ*. The impact of Jesus' teaching is indirectly studied in the lives of other people and the reader makes contact with it only through these interpreters. The trial itself, for all its centrality, takes place off stage and is discussed in retrospect. This pattern of presentation may have certain advantages, and the personality in the wings remains the dominant reality. But it may be conjectured that perhaps it all arises from that uncertainty within Islam as to just where the substitution, discussed above, chronologically begins (though it is the actual personal Jesus to the point of the disciples final, bewildered inquiry). A few incidental difficulties of chronology are apparent at this point. It is difficult also to fit in the progress of Mary Magdalene towards conversion and still leave sufficient time for her lover's conversion and his martyrdom simultaneously with the Cross, after the interlude of the siege and his trial for treachery.

But these are slight matters covered by artistic liberty. Of quite urgent importance, however, is the ultimate question which the author, with the approval of Muslim reviewers, believes lies outside the scope of his work and his intention. It is the question as to who the actual sufferer on the Cross, around whom the parties gather in the final scene, can be held to be. While the heinousness and representative nature of the will to crucify are, as we have argued, in no way affected by this question as to who suffers its implementation, the ultimate meaning of the whole event is undoubtedly involved. Is it finally possible to see the will of the perpetrators, to have the Teacher crucified, so inclusive and significant and not feel the same about the issue as to what happened to Him for Whom they meant this verdict? Is not the entire moral significance, here so movingly argued, spiritually jeopardised, perhaps in a way evaporated, if the encounter never really happened?

The question takes us not only to the heart of this history but to the heart of theology. Jesus' devotion and readiness to die arose from His fidelity to His message, and this in turn from His relationship with God. Is God then properly to be thought of as frustrating the climax of that devotion? Does Jesus, insisting as He does upon loyal obedience unto death, remain the valid spokesman of a Heaven that intervenes to save Him when He would not save Himself? If God, as the Quranic hypothesis affirms, saw that climax differently, had Jesus seen it rightly? Is a love that suffers to the uttermost the truly Divine pattern of wrong's retrieval and humanity's peace with God? Or is the really Divine thing the attitude of self-saving which runs flatly counter to the heart of the teaching of the Sermon? Or in crude brevity: On which side is Heaven? The answer involves the triangular situation that exists both in this book and in the history that generates Christianity, between Jesus, His contemporary opponents and the Divine will. It would appear to the Christian that the whole logic of *City of Wrong* is that the mind of Jesus is the mind of God. To believe Him rescued at the last, while a sufferer, innocent of His role in the world, expires in His stead, is not only an anticlimax. It jeopardises the integrity of a single whole, the totality of the whole Christ in His import for humankind. What is this darkness in which the world is darkened during the three hours of a Friday afternoon? Is it, or is it not, a darkness in which love is redemptively at grips with sin? Or a darkness in which a mistake of identity works out its bitter way before an onlooking Heaven? Only when the shadows that remain around this question are dispelled does the darkness itself become luminous. Yet to be reverently and wistfully within those shadows, as the author and his kinship of readers are, is to be 'on holy ground'.

To kindle such spiritual kinship is the hope of this translation which it has been a joy to attempt. A few final points about translation may therefore be pardoned. Anybody knows, it is no easy art. The aim should be to produce something which does not read like a translation. Yet how to do so without sacrificing a flavour and a feel that go inseparably with language?

In this work, a few basic terms have given me frequent pause. *Da'wah* means literally 'call' but covers in a sense the whole message, mission and meaning-cum-invitation of Jesus. The word

*Fitnah* has already been noted; it is 'sedition,' 'foul wrong,' 'conspiracy' or 'adversity.' At times a phrase or circumlocution seemed necessary. The same is true of *kafara* and its derivatives. Its participle means the 'unbeliever,' the one who denies the faith. But its whole context suggests a rejection of truth in the widest sense, a posture of studied violation, or defiance of the light of truth, of which even the orthodox are in moral senses capable. Then, as well as *Zulm*, there is that awkward customer, *Nizám*. In a Roman military context it implies 'discipline'. Elsewhere it has rather to do with law, the established order of things, the authority by which regimes and systems impose themselves, or 'system' itself, considered as that which exacts and commands the allegiance of men in political or ecclesiastical servitude. The footnotes, which have been added by the translator, are meant to amplify or elaborate points of interest behind the translation. The sub-title has also been supplied, with the author's approval. Opinion in Egypt has recognised the great merit of *City of Wrong* and it was awarded the State Prize for Literature in Cairo in 1957. A noted French orientalist and thinker has recently said of it: 'Cette oeuvre me parait se situer au triple confluent du positivisme scientifique, de la réalité orientale et d'un humanisme universel.' Translations into several languages are in progress, and it is to be expected that these, like the original in Egypt, will stir much thought, and serve to inter-religious meeting in the deepest realms.

If this English version contributes, despite its flaws, to that end, it will have justified itself. It is needless to add that any inexactitudes of meaning or expression are to be laid at my door. They can perhaps be forgiven in the common concern, of Muslim and Christian, critic or reader, author and English-er, for a deeper awareness of man and woman, their undoing and their remaking, in the *Qaryah Zálimah* of our contemporary humanity.

KENNETH CRAGG
JERUSALEM

& 2. Friday

# Friday

The day was a Friday.

But it was quite unlike any other day.

It was a day when certain men went very grievously astray, so far astray in fact that they involved themselves in the utmost iniquity. Evil overwhelmed them and they were blind to the truth, though it was as clear as the morning sky. Yet for all that they were people of religion and character and most careful about following the right. They were endeared to the good and none were given to profounder meditation. They were of all people most meticulous, tenderly affected towards their nation and their fatherland, sincere in their religious practice and characterised by fervour, courage and integrity. Yet this thorough competence in their religion did not save them from wrongdoing, nor immunise their minds from error. Their sincerity did not guide them to the good. They were a people who took counsel among themselves, yet their counsels led them astray. Their Roman overlords, too, were masters of law and order, yet these proved their undoing. The people of Jerusalem were caught that day in a vortex of seducing factors and, taken unawares amid them, they faltered. Lacking sound and valid criteria of action, they foundered utterly, as if they had been a people with neither reason nor religion.

On that day the Jewish people conspired together to require from the Romans the crucifixion of Christ, so that they might destroy his message. Yet what was the mission of Christ save to have men and women be governed by their conscience in all they did and thought? When they resolved to crucify him it was a decision to crucify the human conscience and extinguish its light. They considered that reason and religion alike laid upon them obligations that transcended the dictates of conscience. They did not realise that when people suffer the loss of conscience there is nothing that can replace it. For human conscience is a torch of the light of God and without it there is no guidance for humankind. When humanity has no conscience to guide it every virtue collapses, every good turns to evil and all intelligence is crazed. Persons in this state resemble a dark city, whose familiar haunts and buildings, when the moon is high, give a sense of direction to the inhabitants and show them the way they are going. But when the moon sets, these imposing structures are obstacles and fine signposts are stumbling blocks which simply invite collision and profit the pedestrian nothing. So men and women in life. When conscience illumines them their virtues are true. But when conscience is darkened even their very intelligence and goodness go bad on them.

On that day certain men willed to murder their conscience and that decision constitutes the supreme tragedy of humanity. That day's deeds are a revelation of all that drives us into sin. No evil has ever happened which does not originate in this will of ours to slay our conscience and extinguish its light, while we take our guidance from elsewhere. There is no evil afflicting humanity which does not derive from this besetting desire to ignore the dictates of conscience. The events of that day do not simply belong to the annals of the early centuries. They are disasters renewed daily in the life of every individual. Men and women to the end of time will be contemporaries of that memorable day, perpetually in danger of the same sin and wrongdoing into which the inhabitants of Jerusalem then fell. The same darkness will be theirs until they are resolute not to transgress the bounds of conscience.

# 3. In Jewry

# The Mountain Top

When that day dawned, none of the people of Jerusalem knew that through successive ages it would be universally remembered. It was just one of the spring days the folk in Palestine knew so well. The sun was hardly up before they were getting themselves ready for the familiar tasks of the everyday. The shepherds were early astir leading their flocks to the green pastures around the ancient city. For the capital was ringed with hills of easy access, where the wayfarer could climb without encountering precipitous or rough ground. There were quiet valleys down into which the shepherds made their gentle blissful way. The landscape had no forbidding harshness. Into remotely lying pastures the shepherds would go until the sun's heat became oppressive. Then they would take a siesta under the few surrounding trees, as is the way with shepherds day after day, year by year, century upon century. There are those who think that a shepherd's life is a listless one that enervates his power of thought and atrophies his intelligence. But the real truth is that it is a life which, under the rich benison of God's light, schools them in patience and forbearance and in the love of unhurried meditation and deep reflection, whereby shepherds may attain to the utmost wisdom.

Among those to go out that morning was a young girl whose ragged clothes spoke clearly of poverty. The flock of sheep she drove were partly speckled and partly not. With shepherds such details are significant. The Bible relates how God blessed Jacob's speckled flocks. Leaving the Mount of Olives with its fertile grazing to those who had larger flocks or could give a better account of themselves if it came to a tussle, the girl kept on her casual way until she reached a hill called Calvary, whose top was called Golgotha, or Al-Jumjuma, a lonely place on whose barren rock nothing grew. Bones lay scattered around and waste wood was strewn about. There was a single tree. The sheep themselves had a better instinct for shepherding than this youthful shepherdess and many of them wandered on to where there was better grazing. She did her best to retrieve each wanderer but grew tired with her efforts and, finally, worn out and in despair, she sought shade under the single tree. At noontide the sheep returned to where she sat, seeking shade also, and slept around her. The little shepherdess had only to while away the time until sunset. That was how it was every day. She was blissfully ignorant of what would be taking place that very evening only a few steps from where she slept so peacefully.

The city folk, however, were not accustomed to such early rising as the shepherds, and most of them went out rather sluggishly to the market and the shops. They were by nature a very contentious and argumentative people in all that had to do with them, whether important or not. There was the liveliest discussion that morning. A man would hardly meet his neighbour before they were engaged in conversation about what had transpired the day before in their house of assembly. Most of them regarded the decision of their learned leaders as a right one, without a doubt.

Nevertheless, persons of thought among them were dismayed at the night's proceedings with its heated debate and altercation over this heresy-monger, whose heresy had put an end to their peace. For he had started proclaiming a new religion which increasingly disqualified their convictions and deceived their people. They sensed in his message a menace both to their religion and their way of life. They accordingly had condemned him to be crucified. The house of assembly had agreed together that they would communicate on Friday to their Roman overlords their considered decision relating to the new prophet.

# The Prosecutor

He was among the more prominent public figures in Jewry, this young man whose job was the prosecution of lawbreakers. His family was one of the most notable and eminent and had produced the largest number of doctors of the law. Though still in the prime of life he was already outstandingly successful. But such was the esteem of his family through the generations that people were not envious of him, but loved and admired him. He was known as the most fortunate of men. His wife, whom he had only lately married, was the most beautiful bride in Jerusalem and of a highly favoured family. He was greatly in love with her and she held him tenderly in honour. She customarily slept well into the forenoon, as is the habit of women who spend their evenings in luxury and pleasure. But contrary to her practice she had the idea of rising early this particular day in order to talk with her husband. She wanted something from him and he knew what it was. He would have anticipated her desire but for the notion he had that it might be well to put her off awhile so that she would be obliged to bring all her charms to bear upon him. His idea was quickly justified, for after a little she started the conversation with the remark:

'Today is my birthday.'

'Do you imagine I would forget that?'

'Well, won't you make it a day I'll never forget?'

'Indeed, why not?'

'I want you to be wholly mine today: no other things must keep you busy.'

'Nothing would have made me happier, had it not been for what's going to happen in Jerusalem today.'

'That's nothing to do with me: I'd rather you didn't look round for excuses. I won't allow you an atom's weight of them in what has to do with your love to me.'

'I can't bear you to have the least suspicion I might not come through over something you wanted done. But I have a job on hand today in the hall of assembly. What a job!'

'What's happening in the hall of assembly today?'

'They are demanding the blood of a man against whom the whole people have risen up – populace and priests and doctors of the law. His case must be settled today.'

'What has all that to do with me? Are you of the opinion that the death of some common man calls for your attention more than your love for me? Many men they crucify every day, but today's my birthday: it comes only once a year.'

'It may well be that to the end of time there'll never be a crucifixion such as this prophet's.'

'What is it you want to get him for?'

'I listed against him yesterday enough crimes to set the whole of Jewry against him. My indictment of his crimes makes it perfectly evident that there can be no question of clemency or mercy. They have accordingly condemned him to be crucified. How the people admired my eloquence! – congratulating me on the zeal I showed for the faith, my care for the nation and erudition in the law. There is no doubt that I will follow up this success of yesterday with another triumph today: there must be no weakening of resolve and no drawing back.'

'Success is still your ultimate idol. It makes you its prey and destroys all your good points.'

'It is my love for you that gives me the will to succeed. You women don't care a fig for people who fail.'

'If success means you're no longer wholeheartedly ours, we'll truly be indifferent about it. I am afraid that you may have got to that stage already in your success. What is it has impelled you to this violent prosecuting ardour? Was it love of success or were you sincere? What do you know about him, so to stir up your nation against him? Are you in a frenzy over him?'

'He wants to make the ignorant crowd like we are. He seeks to put the poor on an equality with ourselves. Such ideas are destructive of the whole Jewish order of things. Do you relish being the equal of that blacksmith who works outside your house?'

'I don't see that you have any advantage over him save for the fact that I am your wife and he does not have a wife like me. Any way I do not see that his being made equal to you constitutes a crime for which to crucify people.'

'But more, he has denied God and belied the Divine attributes as they are in the law. He does not talk about God's might and vengeance: all he says is that God is love. He wants people not to fear God but rather to love Him because He loves them. Therein he violates the teachings of the holy law, which can only lead to confusion.'

'Would you kill a man who said that God was love. That's something no criminal would say. God is love!'

'Truly how charming you are! Your gentle beauty suffuses even your errors with sweetness. There's something quite uniquely delightful even about the way you misunderstand things. Do you suppose that the love he is talking about has anything to do with the love of woman? He does not know a thing about women.'

'A woman loves the man who understands love more than she loves the man who understands only women. Most of the latter type are mere hypocrites. The love of woman is the first step to the love of God.'

'I don't know a single man who passed from love of women to love of God.'

'That may be true of men. But women have gone forward from human love to love of God.'

'The knowledge women have of love is not the same as men's. Men love women: but as for women what they love is simply to see themselves the loved of a man. Women like to see themselves in mirrors. These are the men they love.'

'Indeed you have a curious idea of women. Is this how you think of me? Do you consider that my love is what has deterred you from the love of God?'

'How addicted you are to your old mistaken ways. You make every conversation we have together on however general a topic hark back in your mind to our mutual relationship, back to you and me. Love fills your women's hearts. But not so with men. Women live for nothing but love whereas a man has also his mind and his work to think about.'

'Do you think that reason is invariably cool and detached?'

'There may sometimes be a doubt about that. But none the less it is a well-known fact that wise men are above emotion.'

'Intellectual detachment anyway is not the highest good. It seems to me you are greatly changed since yesterday. Your heart used to throb for other things than reason and wisdom. Can that be traced, do you think, to the success you have attained?'

'The summits of high mountains are always covered in snow.'

'For my part I much prefer the lower valley where it is warm. You can go up by yourself where the snows are.'

Then each of them lapsed into silence, her head lying on his breast. Then raising it she looked hard at him. He was different from the man she knew. In a twinkling it came to her that he whom she had loved was changed. She fancied she would leave him. He was aware what she was thinking. The rift that had crept in between them distressed him. He was desperately concerned about her, dreading that his play with words and thought had made her doubtful of him. This was the last thing he had meant. She too realised that her thoughts had gone too far and that what had happened had not affected his love for her. With returning composure she said:

'I realise well enough what your duty is and what you have in hand today. I release you from any preoccupying thoughts about me and my birthday.'

'Now I am re-assured of your intelligence and sound judgement. I had been on the point of protesting this anger of yours. Yet such is our relationship that somehow I find you more attractive when you are aroused than when you are placid. None the less I fail to understand why you should be cross today. Tomorrow we'll be the happiest of people and what's one day in a love which I'm sure is as real as love ever was.'

'Tomorrow will soon be here and you will have brought to

victory religion and nation as well as sound morals.'

'Now my heart's at peace. Soon I'll come back to you and love you as I promised and sweet it will be.'

He wanted to kiss her but she gently turned away her face. He kissed her forehead. But the cold sweat he felt there as he did so plunged him into deep agitation.

He left the house with a much diminished confidence in himself. He was no longer satisfied about the opinions he had held the day before as to his having done his duty perfectly. He was no longer certain that he had been on the side of the truth when by his eloquence he had prevailed upon the people to demand the blood of that strange man.

As for his wife, the sudden change in her emotions had left her exhausted. Love was for her the path to happiness: through love she found her pleasure. Love grew with her satisfaction at the pleasures of life and these in turn increased with love. In this double progression she had been the happiest creature alive. Then came this birthday – the day she had hoped would be the happiest of all. But this business about a man being crucified that day had come between her and her joys. Talk of him had filled her heart so that she had forgotten about herself, which was a new thing in her experience.

God is love! It was a notion which did not lower Divinity but rather ennobled love. The God of the Jews was mighty and terrible: good or evil alike might take their rise in Him. But the God this man preached could only be good. And they'll crucify him today for having denied God. The only thing he has denied is their idea of God. They will kill him because he has committed the crime of saying that God is love. But none but a gracious angel could say such a thing. Would I could go to the place where they want to kill him and look into the face of this man who says that God is love. Who knows? I might surrender myself then to this new love. I would be deceiving myself if I tried to ignore this new light that bathes me. It could well spoil for me the love I have relished hitherto. Perhaps from today on I'll no longer find it good to be merely an attractive loving woman or a passionate wife. Does my husband reckon I'll remain just as he took me yesterday? Then I loved him in a very natural way with a quiet, rational kind of love. But today I am in a fever: and men don't understand women when love grows fierce and fevered within them. Then they are too vehement and urgent in their temper and emotion to submit to reason or to wisdom or hold to one course. The fever of love makes women restless and fickle. It makes them liable to sudden anger with their lovers and prone to abandon their affection for their erstwhile darlings, giving themselves over, even against their will or desire, to some new passion. Let men beware of women when love's ardour burns strong in them. Men are not naturally good at detecting its assaults.

Meanwhile the prosecutor set out for the hall of assembly. He was much pre-occupied with thoughts of himself and beset with doubts about the validity of his stern indictment of a man who had committed no crime and preached nothing damnable. He recalled his remarks of the day before about the man's being an occasion of insurrection and schism within Jewry. He had argued that what the preacher taught threatened their nation's way of life, since their whole existence rested on veneration of their Scriptures, their religion and their traditions. He had emphasised that their religion had become their shield against the menace of fragmentation to which they had been exposed ever since the Romans occupied their country and that the preservation of their religion was their one remaining hope in life. All this he reviewed again in his mind to re-assure himself that he had really taken up the right attitude over the new preaching. He thought that his composure had returned. But in fact he had merely fortified himself with the hedge of his old arguments where he would be immune from the pricks of conscience and the pursuit of bothersome doubts.

# A Blacksmith's Shop

In front of the house, whence this distinguished spokesman of the faith took his departure en route to the hall of meeting, stood a small dirty shop belonging to a poor blacksmith. Duty, as the learned man saw it, to himself, his religion and his learning, obliged him to ignore this poor, ignorant neighbour. This had nothing to do with vanity or pompousness on his part. He sincerely believed that the business of the world would only go right when people were divided into classes, each of which reverenced the class that was superior in rank and learning. It would not have entered his head to linger by this workshop but for his conversation with his wife when it had been mentioned, and but for the fact that he noticed a merchant in front of it, who, livid with rage, was raining down blows on the blacksmith. He was bawling so loudly that he might well have choked as he said:

'Where is the work you promised me yesterday? Where are the four big nails I ordered you to make? What's your furnace doing with no fire there? Do you realise what your negligence will bring upon me? I'll be breaking my promise with the Roman authorities. Never before has such a thing happened in my dealings with them. If that occurs today I will forfeit their confidence in me – confidence the very thing I am most proud about. The confidence men have in them is the secret of the success of the sons of Israel. People know us for goodness, reliability and integrity, virtues we have inherited from our fathers. We can't have the likes of you alienating people from us by flouting these virtues. No stupid ignorant fool like you should be in a position to do your nation harm this way. Your laziness will be your own undoing also. You'll take the provender from your family and reduce them to beggary. It's easy enough for me to abandon you and go elsewhere. In fact I know a blacksmith upon whom I'll lavish so much wealth that he'll be in clover while you lie in a hell of poverty. Yet, for all that, I want to be kind with you. I'll double your wages, on condition you get your fire going and begin operations right away. There's no more time to be lost. Take this money; there'll be more for you when things are under way.'

The blacksmith took the money and was on the point of throwing it into the depth of the furnace when the man rushed at him and, rescuing his money, shouted:

'What are you doing? Are you mad? There must be something wrong with you, to damage yourself, your people, your nation and your trade in this fashion! Can't you say what's wrong with you ?'

The blacksmith made no reply and seeing him adamant the other tried to enlist in his aid a man with a long beard who had been sitting for some time at the door of the shop, with downcast eyes and a grave expression. He seemed heedless for the most part of what was going on around him. He was carrying a large key which he did not put down.

At the first glance the merchant remembered that the man was one of the principal followers of the new prophet. He suspected that he was the one who had forbidden the blacksmith from making the articles he had ordered from him, since he knew that they were wanted in preparation of the cross on which his prophet and leader was to die. He knew the big nails were meant for his hands and feet.

'Now the mystery that puzzled me is clear enough. Isn't it this stupid fellow who has asked you to desist from making what I gave you command about? He's the one who has told that it's all intended for the making of a cross for his leader to die on? He's even more stupid and despicable than you are yourself. Nothing makes me madder than the stupid folly that leads you and him to think that the sons of Jewry with all their intelligence, zeal and wisdom, will ever fall for the likes of you and him. I've no illusions that you'll understand what I'm going to say but nevertheless I'm going to give you a piece of my mind. Listen to me: If this man is a liar then his death is entirely right, and nobody can question it. As for the possibility that he is genuine and his being put to death a gross injustice, you can be sure I've reckoned with that for a long time. Concede if you will that his murder would be a great crime incurring God's retribution: we are still secure from it. I know what's going to be done with the iron, but I am not making it. I am only buying and selling it. God will not punish me for buying and selling. There's nothing about that in the holy law. You make the iron but you have nothing to do with what it is used for as long as you know nothing about it. I do not even touch it with my own hand; I shall be sending it to the Romans by a lad who knows nothing. He will not be punished for what he does. Don't you see? When the greatest crimes are shared out among a number of people it becomes impossible for God to bring retribution upon a single one of the perpetrators. We can prove that from the sacred law. It is not permissible to contradict what is found in the Book.

'Moreover, if he who is aware that what's going on is a crime does not fashion the instruments for it, and if he who makes the instruments knows nothing of the crime, then it can easily be accomplished. This spreading of responsibility puts people off the scent, as to where the Divine retribution will fall. Thus the greatest crimes are committed without punishment. Don't you see that neither God nor men repay any single person for the atrocities which are done in time of war — atrocities which strike terror into the hearts of all who hear tell of them — after the heat of passion during hostilities has abated. There is no retribution from God or men for these crimes because they are committed in the name of society, and because the guilt they involve is distributed in such a way as to make retributory punishment an injustice if it is visited on any single individual. It isn't fitting for God to inflict wrong on anyone. Retribution validly falls on individual guilt but this spreading of the onus makes it too tiny for anyone to care about. I wonder if you're taking anything in of what I say?'

At this point in the harangue the blacksmith would have rushed on the merchant with a hammer, one blow of which would have killed him instantly, but he was restrained from his purpose by the prosecutor who stood in the shop doorway. The pair of them looked at this devil of a man and sent him off. He withdrew from them with angry contemptuous glances.

As the prosecutor listened to the conversation he was seized with trembling and the colour went from his cheeks. Was he too among those who participated in great sin by partial sharing so that no one, not even the God of Israel Himself, would know whose was the due retribution? He pondered long on what this devil incarnate had said and then began soliloquising:

'The conscience of the individual does not forbid society from committing the greatest of crimes, so long as they are committed in the name of society. Conscience is the only factor restraining us from evil, and societies have no conscience. None of the individuals within them are troubled in conscience by what his community perpetrates, however great an iniquity it be. Look at what happens in war. Those who have news of a war when the business is over have very confused reactions to what happens, though war involves things that are utterly intolerable to conscience, however hardened and coarsened it may be. Probably not a single combatant in the two warring sides would approve the war in which he fights if he consulted with his own conscience alone. But society as a whole goes out to war with an easy and undisturbed attitude – may even greet it with relish and delight. It is all very incomprehensible and irrational. I have never before been able to understand it. But what I have just heard elucidates the contradiction. A criminal thing, however evidently so, can be committed readily enough if it is so shared as to make the implication of the individual in its guilt so trifling that it ceases to trouble his conscience.

'Did we not hear of a commander whose army routed the enemy? He wanted to exact vengeance on all the prisoners. So he ingeniously suggested putting out the eyes of all of them, with the exception of one man at the head of every hundred who would be left with one eye to take charge of the rest. Had he himself been personally in charge of putting into effect this torture his decision would have terrified him. If the judge who pronounces sentence of execution were responsible for carrying it out, he might have a different idea about the value of the evidence. The commander who orders his army to indiscriminate slaughter only gives the word. Others do the killing. When in olden times the prophets were slain this was the way in which their deaths were brought about. They were so shared out among the whole community that the only real murderer was the community.' Then he began to think of a way out of the whole thing and felt a little more at ease.

'The individual conscience is the most potent factor inducing us towards the good. It is in fact the sole means of guidance into truth. But when vital questions are put to it it errs and grows confused and bewildered. Then it has to decide between two courses of action each of which has an aspect of the truth.'

But as he went on ruminating, his despair and distress returned. 'When the sacred law discusses good and evil they are as plain as can be. There's nothing dubious about them at all. I used to think that they could never be confused. But I no longer now distinguish them as clearly as I used to do. I used to listen to my grandfather who was an eminent doctor of the law saying that he no longer knew the difference between good and evil. They had become, he said, so intermingled in his mind that he could not tell precisely where the dividing line between them came. I remember considering that such remarks were a bit of empty boasting on his part, as if he meant to imply that he was above the good and evil of ordinary folk. I regarded this superior attitude as a deficiency in him. Indeed I actually took it as an indication of the fact that when a person has a mature intelligence they may have less feeling for others. I took his remark as evidence of the enfeeblement that had befallen him in his old age. Could it be that I too have now reached the same stage of feebleness, though I am still in the bloom of youth? May it be that discriminating between good and evil, or between truth and falsehood, is very much the same as distinguishing between what is beautiful and what is ugly, namely that it depends on whether you are near to them or far removed. Don't you agree that the most beautiful and the least beautiful women are all very much alike if you see them from the summit of a mountain? Equally they're alike if you look at them so closely that you do not see more than, say, a finger tip. Perhaps it is our close proximity to what happened yesterday which prevents us from seeing whether it is right or wrong. Our fathers worshipped the calf which we regard as the grossest of errors. But being so close to it in time they did not see it that way at all. Caesar has no conception of the difference between the three men to be crucified today, for the reason that he is so far from them in station. And we make no distinction between them because we are so close to them. Will what is good today be evil ten years hence and become good again after twenty years? Will what we here regard as good be seen by people in Rome as being evil? Where is good? Where is evil? They both seem very much alike unless we are at a particular remove from them in time and in space. What exactly is this remove? And beyond or after that, what remains of the sanctity of good?'

His thoughts left him quite giddy and he went around to the house of a friend whom he drew into conversation about the things he had seen and heard and all that had passed through his mind since the morning began. There was no mistaking his agitation as he said:

'I had no idea we had among us such a fellow as this merchant. Even Satan himself could not have decked the deeds of evil with more plausibility than that chap's remarks did. He tells people that they are quite secure from sin and punishment so long as they spread the wrongdoing out among them.'

'Don't be extravagant in your reproach of your nation. The people of Israel are a microcosm of humanity, and can be distorted just as people are when they walk in front of those concave and convex mirrors. You know how part of the body gets grossly magnified while the other is reduced to the tiniest proportions. Then when people move away the huge part grows minute and the minute looms large. Israel is like that. She has within herself all the aspects of humanity, both good and bad. Only sometimes her virtues look big while her vices are negligible. At other times these virtues diminish while the vices are magnified. There is nothing new about us: we merely reproduce in this respect the character of all peoples.'

'Anyway, there is one thing I am anxious to know. Are we right in prosecuting this man and in having him crucified? — or are we wrong?'

'Let your conscience be your sole court of appeal. It is your conscience which is to guide you.'

'It is not a matter for conscience alone. It depends more largely on reason. And my reason gives me the feeling that there is real danger to Jewry in his message. It was because of this that I demanded his blood. But I would like to be sure whether he is truly a menace to us. I want to know where reason is taking us. Is it along the road of truth or of delusion?'

'There's no way of knowing, if reason is to be your only guide. Has the ant any capacity to know whether it is ascending up to the top of the hill or descending down into the depth of the valley? Because of its shortness of sight and its tiny steps it is the most meticulous of all God's creatures in what it does. It is competent for the wrong and the right that are close at hand. It is not concerned about remote objectives.'

'But people are not ants. By dint of their reason they peer into the distant scene.'

'And that is precisely where their greatest blunders arise. They suppose themselves capable of seeing into the future intelligently. They imagine they can set in motion factors conducing to particular ultimates. Yet that whole estimate of things is through and through mistaken. If only they would order things on the basis of the dictates of their conscience in the present, and not be so excessively confident about their rational delineation of distant consequences, they would make far fewer mistakes.'

'Even the most intelligent people are unaware what consequences their actions may have one year or ten years hence. Those who make calculations of this sort will continue to fumble and stumble in the darkness of error. You heard did you not about that building the Egyptians and Greeks were expert at? It consisted of labyrinthine paths. Anybody who went in had the utmost difficulty in finding his way out, unless he had a guide to show him. When the wanderer inside came to a crossroad, he had no means of knowing whether he was right or wrong. Life is like that. No one knows when they choose a particular path whether they are on the way to success or failure, whether what they are doing is right or wrong.'

'What concerns me is that I have right guidance on this simple issue: Is the crucifixion of this man today right or wrong?'

'Decide by your conscience alone and then follow it sincerely. Then there'll be no need to query whether people a hundred years hence will approve what you did. In any event we have no way of knowing about that.'

'My conscience left to itself can see nothing to lay to his charge.'

'Well, shall we say so today?'

'I would that I could bring about his deliverance.'

He lapsed into silence for a while and so did his interlocutor. Then the conversation was resumed.

'Would you not like to take my place today and call upon the people to reverse their decision of yesterday? It would be easier for you to do it.'

'I should think I'd be much more anxious to get guidance for myself than to offer it to others. My view is that people should only undertake responsibility for public affairs when their personalities are mature and their dispositions stable. They should themselves be calm and self-possessed as well as free from taint so that they do not visit their own ill humours on the people. And thus far I have developed no such propensities. Those who have a role to play in public life must first have rid themselves of the troubles of their private lives. I have not yet achieved that, so any effort I might expend in public life would do me little credit.'

'Doesn't it attract you to wield power over others and to know that you take precedence over them? Doesn't it appeal to you to be the arbiter both of force and clemency just as if you had become God's deputy over His creation? Does not success allure you? Or do you not find your soul urging you into passions that take you beyond the bounds of reason? Let me congratulate you on this contentedness that fills your heart and on the way you hold aloof from impulses to self-gratification and indulgence of desire. As for me, when I contend with people and get the better of them or can exercise authority over them, I feel that selfishness is the prime motive. My distress about this is sharpened when I talk with people like you who have not been seized by such egotism.'

'Well let's suppose for argument's sake that it is selfishness which takes you into the public service. What's egotistical about that? Taking religious vows has many more selfish features, however exacting and austere it may be. For the only purpose the monk has is to benefit his own soul, either here in this world or in the other. His celibate existence profits no one but himself. So since you have congratulated me on my contentedness, I'm going to felicitate you on your keen sense of life and your urge to participate in it fully. Seeing that a quiet existence is not in accord with your nature you would only be miserable if you were to aspire towards it. And even if people like me were pushed into strife, it would only mean wretchedness, being foreign to our temperament.'

'But, pursuing my own self-satisfaction and achieving my own security, I may be doing harm, or good, who knows? I may be in the wrong, or I may be right, perhaps injuring the innocent and promoting evil doers. I may do all those things simply in going after the enjoyment of my deep passion for life.'

'Yet, whether you're at fault or in the right, in any case your service to the public is on your part a worthy thing. People like you who take life competitively thereby take it strenuously. Nobody with those ideas on life is ever content with anything or satisfied with himself, even if he acquires the authority of the Caesars. And as far as selfishness is concerned, would there really be much difference the other way? Suppose they were to reconcile themselves to the idea that life is not competitive but that it consists in realising one's innate powers and potentialities, and suppose they were sure their one duty was not to fall short in achieving what they were made for, with all their natural aptitudes both strong and weak, then all they would need to make them happy would still thereby be coming to them, namely the struggle to achieve.'

'What you have just said goes far to lighten my pain and distress of soul. Even so I have no desire to go today to the hall of assembly. I don't want to find myself carrying the entire burden.'

With that our friend went out. But actually he was not a whit less restless and bewildered. The conversation had done nothing to allay the rebellion within. Nor had it afforded any guidance on the right path. He began to soliloquise again. The greatest crimes are easily and readily perpetrated, but so long as they are distributed among many the share of each individual is too insignificant for his conscience to bother about. Satan himself could not find a more effective delusion than this to drive people to hell. Am I to follow this path to hell unaware whither my reason and my learning are taking me?

# The Mufti

There was in Jerusalem a devout and learned lawyer, highly revered and loved by his community. He was responsible for the issue of religious fatwas among the Jews, who are a people in perpetual need of such fatwas, or legal opinions. They have an incessant demand for exegesis of the texts of the sacred law whenever it inconveniences their behaviour – a circumstance that very frequently occurs. For example, one of the matters that bothers the religious among them arises from their belief that a man must give a piece of gold as dowry to his bride. If he is so poor that he lacks the wherewithal to do so, they sell him a gold ring for a trifling sum, a dirham or two, and he presents her with it. Then they buy it back from her a few minutes afterwards. This they regard as preferable to letting the poor man forego the gift of gold, since such a permission has no textual support in the holy books. In this way, the custodian of fatwas has a significant role among the Jews and this mufti especially so. For he was most ardent that his fatwas should be right in the sight of God. He had an intelligent son who always accompanied him to the sessions, where he listened and learned. He was preparing to follow in his father's footsteps as a mufti. That morning he was full of vigour and wellbeing, as he saluted his father early, kissing his hand and sitting down beside him, after his daily habit.

'Father, I heard yesterday what the prosecutor said about the man with the new message. How happy I was with that wonderful address, combining as it did the ripest knowledge, a keen intelligence and a spell-binding flow of eloquence. Doubtless you were just as full of admiration as the people were. They listened to him in amazement, hanging on every word he said, as though the excellence of his case had dazed them, not to speak of his undoubted sincerity and his great patriotism. Until today I would not have believed that anyone could have entranced the learned leaders of Israel and captured their hearts and minds like that learned orator did. But most of all it was the force of his argument that I admired. He proceeded in sequence to set out his facts, arranged most wisely and meticulously, beginning with the less significant and working up towards the most serious. When finally he reached the most crucial of all, you could see him appropriately intensifying his style and raising his voice. His contentions followed each other in such a fine logical order that no one could be left in any doubt about the evil character of this new doctrine.

'But even that did not suffice him. He turned to the future of Jewry and gave us an impressive picture, describing what would befall our nation if the people of this generation allowed their power to weaken or anarchy to make its insidious way into our life and our dogmas. He explained to us how the future of the Jewish people a thousand years hence or more would depend upon what we did today. If compassion should take hold of us and we drew back from the fulfilment of our duty, the whole nation of Israel would be destroyed. But if we resisted the heresy, our people two thousand years on would applaud our courage. Though that still lies in the remote unknown, it was all as clear as if one saw it with one's own eyes. Truly intelligence is a Divine light by which we see what will transpire after we and our children and our children's children lie in the dust. Can it be that his views so clearly expounded are in any way faulty?

'Whatever else I forget, I will always remember how he said: The whole life of Israel, nation, religion and order, is a trust in our keeping. We must not allow our nation to be weakened by every purveyor of new heresy. Heresies cannot affect us, however multifarious, for we are too well grounded in the faith to be troubled by what you have heard. But heresy is like an axe striking at a wall. At first it may have no apparent effect on it. Yet unbeknown the blow makes the wall more likely to fall under a further rain of blows. You must cut off the source of this disruptive evil: for such indeed it is. You have it on the mufti's official opinion

– in every way a learned and proper authority – that the miracles of the preacher of the new doctrine are no indication of his authenticity, even if they are established as true. You are aware also of the statement of the head of the learned lawyers to the effect that the ethical principles he preaches, lofty as they may be, run counter to what God Himself has enjoined upon us. Does not God know better what is right for us? Is it tolerable that a man like this should set himself above the very commandments of God, to Whom be praise and honour? He orders his disciples to love their enemies. If we were so artless as to listen to this charming notion, which we cannot pass over in silence, it would be the end of Israel. If we were to believe it, our unity would be dissolved and our corporate personality forfeited. Our nationhood would be annihilated in the midst of the powerful enemies that surround us. That shall never be. Everything we know of him confirms that he is a deceiver of considerable cunning and it is our bounden duty to destroy him. Indeed, I will go further. Grant that he is sincere, grant that he has power and authority, commanding the mountains and they remove and the dead that they rise, grant that he could send out thunderbolts and destroy even us who sit in judgement on him,[3] grant all that as indubitable, veritable fact, yet I summon you in spite of all, flinch not from making away with him! Who among us would refuse to die for the sake of our people Israel's life? What sacrifices shall not be counted little for the sake of a people such as we are and for a religion like ours? Think of Israel two thousand years from now. Give sentence against this preacher of heresy in a manner you and the nation will take pride in at that far off day.

'Was anything so beautiful ever heard or read by mortals?'

His father answered him:

'But is there in the charm of words any proof that the speaker's ideas are valid or his judgement true?'

'We were only going according to your own fatwa and the opinion of the head of the doctors of the law.'

'We both of us know that he borrowed from our remarks just the things he fancied and left aside what did not fit his inclinations. Haven't I warned you that half truth is worse than falsehood?'

'Well, why didn't you think of that yesterday?'

'I'll have it in mind today.'

'That will be of no use. There is a settled conviction among the people that duty requires his being crucified.'

'Is that my wrongdoing?'

'Do you regard it as wrongdoing on the part of the prosecutor?'

'It may not be, and it may not be wrongdoing on the people's part either, for they merely fall in with what their superiors tell them.'

'If what happened yesterday is wrong, who is the culprit?'

'Only God knows.'

'Isn't it possible that what the learned doctors decided yesterday is right?'

'It could just as well be wrong. What's going to happen today could disgrace the people of Israel for ever. It could be utterly disastrous in its consequences for them as a people, a religion and a way of life, for twenty centuries to come. But you can be certain the thunderbolts won't fall on us today, however misguided we may be in what we do. It was a cheap gesture to call for self-sacrifice in the nation's cause and the cause of our life and purity in faith. Though what we are seeking in this decision is to make Jewry secure it could well be that our action will lead to the massacres of Jews in thousands. Hundreds of thousands of our people may suffer for the step to which we are urged by this harangue whose empty periods have so charmed you. And they'll be innocent people whose only crime is this verdict.'

'Doubt is profitless when it supervenes at the moment of action. Is there no means of telling what is the right course in this business?'

'I do not know. What I am certain of in this affair is that there are two ways that take us into error. One is to go back into history for guidance and precedents: the other is in cogitation to anticipate the future and find guidance there. Then we assess the present on the basis of our imaginary foretellings. Perhaps history, though admittedly weak, is a better guide than pretentious soothsaying. For such prognostications are quite unable to validate themselves by proof, however much we may be taken in by the intellectual brilliance that generally goes with them. If you are thinking of how Pharaoh listened with admiration to Joseph's prophecies before he had offered any proof of them, so that Pharaoh's credence and wonder were based only on the tokens of intelligence he found in Joseph's words, you should remember that Joseph's being right in what he said was not because of some rational power of soothsaying, but because he was inspired by God. But those foretellers who are not of the prophets, but rely only on their wits, they are deceivers. They are more often wrong than right.'[4]

'What is for us the way to truth?'

'Leave the unknown to God. We have no way of knowing it. The future is too benighted to be our guide. Let us restrict our judgements to the present which is all we have competence for and let us never transgress the bounds of conscience. Certainly conscience can find no rest in this man's being crucified. Reason in us might, alone, approve it. But conscience in any of us, unless it be tainted by reflective thinking that has gone astray, will never be reconciled to what we are doing.'

Whereupon the boy fell into a gloomy silence. When his mother entered bringing food for them she sensed that there was something out of the ordinary about both of them. His father remarked that he had no desire to eat and the son, too, said that their conversation had taken away all appetite, though he had begun the day so full of zest. When his mother learned what had passed between them she said to her son:

'Your father was made with this malady of doubt and vacillation. I've never known him give an important fatwa without going back on it and wishing to himself: Would I had not done so!'

'I shall give no more fatwas from now on. They have misconstrued the ones I gave and seek by them to murder a man whose death my conscience cannot approve.'

'Perhaps you would like to go back on your opinion today?'

'What's to prevent me doing so? I don't want my fatwa to stay for all time the cause of the crucifixion of one of whom I know no wrong.'

'Isn't it possible that the fatwa was valid?'

'Even so, any benefit that might accrue from its being right is far outweighed by its enormity if it's wrong.'

'Everybody was convinced that his being crucified was a duty. Having heard all that was deliberated on yesterday they will not change their mind. Your change of front will have no effect on them. The common folk do not understand hesitancy, even when doubt is in fact the right attitude. They follow anyone who can assure them that his view is true and indubitable, though it be invalid from start to finish.'

'Let me leave to others the handling of the masses. That's no business of mine. What concerns me is that they should not set up something wrong on an opinion attributed to me. If you want assured truth, search for it in some other world than this or beyond humanity. I do not wish to be a deceiver of the people or be on their behalf a guarantor of particular ideas. I do not wish to misrepresent things to them, though it be for their own good. If you share the opinion that believes deception to be justified in politics, you should be clear that it is only so because politicians have so willed it for their own advantage. They choose the line of least resistance to gain their ends. You see them revelling in prevarication and vying with each other in it, should that be the easiest path to their goal. They could of course gain these objectives by the path of rectitude but it would be much more tedious and troublesome. When men of religion adopt the attitudes of politicians it is because they have set politics above religion, or rather the politics of religion above religion itself. And that is manifest error.'[5]

# Lazarus

A man named Lazarus who had been raised from the dead lived in Jerusalem. His being brought back to life was a miracle that everyone talked about. Only few, however, believed in it. The majority denied it. It was the topic of much debate in the hall of meeting as they deliberated the case of the new prophet, whose followers claimed that he had the power to raise the dead. One thing about which there was no doubt was that Lazarus had been dead some days when his sister sought out Christ and asked him for her sake to bring her brother back to life. She had no other brother in the world. She really believed in Christ and he answered her faith. Life returned to her brother. But those who had known him previously as a handsome, merry and intelligent youth hardly recognised him after his return. He was now pallid complexioned, with sunken eyes. He was taciturn and thought incoherently. No one pondering his features could detect any natural, human emotions. He was neither glad, nor sorrowful: he neither laughed nor wept. But if annoyed by anything he broke into violent anger and at the slightest provocation would become unduly agitated. He lived in perpetual fear, terror evident in his furtive glances, as if he were for all the world like a lion at bay with no way of escape.

  He was on friendly terms with no one, not even with the sister for whose sake he had been raised again. He talked to none of his former friends nor would he sit down with anyone. He kept to the narrow streets when he walked abroad. His sister alone of all the people of Jerusalem sat at his feet, kissed him and held him in affection. She alone took his return to her as a blessing. Losing him had been enough to banish hope from her existence. Now she clung to him as one might to whom a precious trust had been restored when he had thought it lost beyond recall. The general populace in Jerusalem, however, felt his presence to be sinister and reacted to him with uneasy hatred and antagonism. The thought of him troubled everybody: nobody was willing to acknowledge him. None enquired of him what death was like though he alone had tasted it and returned from his experience. Even the disciples of the new prophet had no love for him, nor did they regard him as one of them, despite the fact that they took him for a sign from God and a token of the authenticity of the leader in whom they believed. Everyone agreed that his being raised again was in no sense a blessing either for Lazarus himself or for any of his fellows. They considered him in fact the most wretched person in Jerusalem. It seemed to them that when life returned to him it brought back with it neither spirit nor soul. If, they thought to themselves, our universal dream of returning back to life in this world can only happen in these terms, we are unanimous that there's no good to anyone in such a resurrection.

While Lazarus was out walking early that day some children spotted him. They gathered around and began throwing stones at him, with jeers and taunts. They followed down the narrow alleys which he invariably chose, keeping at a distance when he beat them off and closing up to him when he tried to elude them. In one particular alley down which he went there was a poor blacksmith's shop. Work there was so scant that the blacksmith hardly made enough to eat. But that day he was on top of the world. A well known merchant had paid him a visit and asked him to kindle the furnace fire and make certain articles that had to be finished, as a matter of urgency, that day. It was, he explained, a most important commission, though he was anxious nothing should be said about it.

Rewarding the blacksmith profusely, the merchant stood a little distance away watching the furnace after the fire had been lit and the blacksmith, hammering away amid a crescendo of sparks. He was well content: his promise to the Roman governor would soon be fulfilled.

As Lazarus came up, with the children in pursuit, he took it into his terror-stricken head to seek shelter in the blacksmith's shop. Glancing up as he entered, the smith let out a shriek that struck fear into the heart of the fugitive.

'Get out of here', he yelled, 'You'll never enter this place. The curse you bring is worse than all. I've had enough misery in my life already. Don't bring an evil omen here the very day a ray of hope has dawned for me.'

Beside himself with rage the blacksmith brandished his hammer, and as his hand trembled it flew from his grasp into the furnace. Fragments from the fire flew up in all directions and one struck the merchant in the eye. He bellowed with fright and pain. The blacksmith rushed frenziedly to where the trader stood to see what had happened to him. In doing so he slipped and fell to the ground. There were many nails lying about where he fell and one of them pierced his hand as he struck the ground and came through the palm. In the growing tumult of cries and confusion people came up from all sides to the aid of the two victims. Lazarus, meanwhile, saw his opportunity, took to his heels and, evading his pursuers, found his way to safety. When his two sisters saw him in his state of terror they were overcome with grief and fell to praying and beseeching God to complete His mercy upon Lazarus and give him back health and sanity and beauty once again. God heard their prayer. But Lazarus could no longer bear to live thereabouts. He determined to leave for a far away land and preach there the new religion.

Anxious to re-assure himself that he could still see with the other eye, the merchant took a glance at the blacksmith. There he was, his hand in the air, pierced through with a nail. Despite the unbearable pain, his composure returned and he ceased crying out. He asked the people to conduct him to his house and to take the blacksmith to a doctor, remarking to his friends that he wanted to take his injury uncomplainingly. There was something in his mind he did not wish to reveal that they were not aware of. There was a healing of his spirit in the pain of his body – healing from a malady of which none but he knew.

Meanwhile where it had all happened a great crowd

accumulated as the hubbub and the uproar mounted. Cries were raised demanding vengeance on the sorcerers who were corrupting everything and tormenting the innocent. When the merchant heard what they were saying he asked them to disperse. He wanted no revenge: nor did he believe that what had befallen him was the work of the new prophet's followers. The mob, however, sensed their power and vowed vengeance, asserting that if those disciples cured the sick they could as well bring sickness on the able-bodied. Those who brought the dead to life could also murder the innocent. They shouted among themselves: 'Let us go to the hall of assembly and demand the blood of the whole gang, his and his followers.'

Then they caught sight of a man in their midst who was physically too weak to go with them through all the motions of vindictive zeal. Taking this circumstance as proof that he disavowed their intent, they set about him and beat him. When he fainted a bystander spoke up: 'This is a crime; you're killing an innocent man who has done no wrong.' The crowd turned on him with looks of sadistic hatred and cried out angrily: 'Here's another of his disciples. Kill him.' As they bore down on him the man went deathly pale. To confront an angry mob is like facing a beast of prey. Those who were nearest to him shied one by one away from his glance. But the crowd itself was not daunted and had almost lynched him, guiltless as he was, but for the timely intervention of men who knew him well and rescued him from their clutches. Ever after that he had an implacable hatred of milling crowds. Full well he knew that they have no sense of truth, reason or justice. Force is the only thing they recognise and acknowledge.

One of the most inveterate adversaries of the prophet with the new message and his adherents, a learned doctor of Israel, arrived at the merchant's house. On hearing about these events he was only too ready to take it for a certainty that there was further proof here of how bad this faction was. No good could possibly come of it. He went aside with the merchant and asked him the truth about the strange incident.

'I myself don't find anything specially remarkable about it. I

# In Jewry

was standing beside the fire and should have kept at a safe distance. Had I done so nothing would have befallen me. When an iron hammer fell into the fire the sparks flew out and struck my eye. What's strange about that? Then a man fell on the ground and a nail went through his hand. Isn't that natural enough? Why do you want to analyse and interpret what occurred so tediously?'

'But this fellow who was raised after he was dead, wasn't he passing by just at the moment when it happened? You surely know this man is at the back of every damned thing these days. He's the source of divisions in Israel and people have a fear and dread of seeing him. His appearance alone is enough to show that his resuscitation was the work of Satan. The breath that breathes in him has nothing of God about it. It is the breath of evil. He's alive but he hasn't lost yet the features of death. It's as if life has returned into him so that he has an animal existence but hasn't attained to being man again.'

'Is there nobody to give him the benediction of their friendship, nobody glad to take him by the hand in token of goodwill? Or has God not done uniquely for him what He has done for none other in the world?'

'I think no one but his sister considers him favoured of God. She almost worships him, though the disciples, even, have no friendly dealings with him. They don't sit down together except when they want to prove the truth and power of their prophet.'

'For my part I don't understand what makes people so suspicious and apprehensive. Can it be that this being raised again has some special significance?'

'I was listening when our chief scribe mentioned him one day. This is what he said: He is a symbol of a person's conscience after they have committed some transgression and repented. God relents towards us after our wrongdoing. He restores to us our conscience after it has been awhile dead. For to sin is to murder one's conscience. But when conscience revives it is only after the fashion of this Lazarus, half alive and half dead. It's impossible for a human conscience to be entirely pure and clean after repentance, as is the conscience of some innocent person who has committed no sin.'

'Only a person well endowed with wisdom and learning would be capable of such a fine idea. The vulgar throng doesn't understand symbol. I'm firmly convinced, anyway, that this man's being around has nothing to do with today's events.'

'People talk of their forebodings. They'll say that what has happened to you is a portent to warn us of what will befall many of us if we are not alerted. Others hold the view that strange events of this sort are generally a Divine punishment meted out on some criminal wrongdoer. But there's no crime we're aware of, either in you or the wretched blacksmith, that would warrant such a punishment as this. Realising as everybody does that both of you are innocent, it seems beyond question that what befell you was the work of Satan. That's what I believe too. I am going to the hall of assembly today to relate this information. I'll put it to them as clear proof that there is a link between these people and the devil and that the latter is using them to torment innocent folk like yourself. There is no blinking the fact that we must get rid of the lot of them.'

'Will you persist in that opinion if I tell you that what happened to us today is a miracle attesting them as trustworthy? If not, let me tell you that the same factors which make you devalidate them compel me to believe in them. This man is possessed of an extraordinary power. I would like you to know, and to make known about me, that I was in that shop making ready the necessary iron for the cross on which their prophet is to be crucified today and to prepare the nails that are to be driven into his hands and feet. The Roman governor had so demanded and I had given him my word on it. I did not want to go back on my word. When I opened my eye and saw the blacksmith waving a nail-pierced hand in the air it clearly seemed to me a symbol of the great crime that is on the point of being done today. The smith was fashioning the instruments of a wicked deed and it seemed like a Divine visitation. With beating heart, I began to believe. I knew that the hand of God was over ours and that this man who belongs to Him was unjustly served.'

His learned friend was amazed and said:

'Is what you say true? You're turning my ideas topsyturvy. Do you think these men can be sincere before God, that they are not the disciples of the devil?'

'That's exactly what there can be no doubt about from now on.' The visitor lapsed into silence at that, his arguments exhausted. He was dubious awhile until his vanity and love of the winning side got the better of him. He feared too what people would say of him and the anger of the populace. Finally he said:

'It's all a figment of your imagination. Do you suppose the whole of Jewry are mistaken merely because you've seen a nail in a blacksmith's hand and had the wild idea that it was a punishment on him for being the maker of nails for the new heretic's crucifixion? With all my experience and intelligence do you think I'm going to follow your fantasies or rate them above the likely views that are mature and sound? God, you think, needs such a sign to convince people that a servant of His is being wronged? Isn't He able to send a thunderbolt down on the lot of us from heaven and make an end of us before we slay His prophet? Is God, in your view, so weak that He cannot prevent the crucifixion of His apostle except by such an outlandish sign? You'll never make any impression on me with such ideas.'

'You have not lost an eye nor had a nail through your hand. Had you gone through what befell me you would have believed.'

'Then you think that God's way of inducing His servants' beliefs is to put out people's eyes and let iron pierce their hands?'

'Yes: this is His way with those who disbelieve or are predisposed to.'

'Then have you any idea what is going to befall me? I'm much more incredulous and sceptical than you were.'

'Verily God guides whom He will, without either token or sign. But others with tokens and signs. But He guides not those for whom He wills perverseness.'[6]

'Truly your idea of God is very naive: like that of stupid ignoramuses who think He looks upon them individually and reckons up their deeds, one by one. That's a kind of notion about

God which anyone would find laughable who has the least knowledge and intelligence. Belief like yours is one of the most compelling reasons for atheism. Atheists would certainly deny such views about His attributes as yours.'

'Well, go on thinking in your intelligent way. For my part, I heard one of his followers saying that dullwittedness, ignorance and poverty were the path to guidance. If you're interested at all in me and what I think, then take it from me – I've forsaken your community for his. From today on, I'm stupid, ignorant and poor.'

They both broke off speaking. The scholar went out in a mood of ugly anger and made for the hall of meeting. In a new access of strength, he determined not to abandon his convictions of the day before, despite an inward feeling that the truth was no longer quite as evident as he had thought it to be an hour ago!

# Caiaphas

When custody of Israel's destinies passed into the hands of Caiaphas, most people rejoiced at the prospect of being ruled by a man who was, at once, learned, just and good. That situation was far from being unprecedented in Jewry. Prophets, judges and kings had ruled over them in earlier ages and some of their kings had been apostles and saints. The Jews had some knowledge of Greek philosophy and were prepared to recognise that the Greeks possessed wisdom even though no book had come to them as revelation from heaven, and their consciences were not schooled by religion. They had heard tell also of the thought of the greatest of Greek thinkers that public affairs should be entrusted to philosophers. Since Caiaphas was, as it were, their philosopher and their Solon, the Jewish people were well content that he should preside over their life. They considered that a new era had opened in their national history and were convinced it would be a happy one.

The Jews found themselves at that juncture in their affairs at a point of unparalleled crisis and trial. It had started when the Romans conquered their country and took it over. The most exacting feature of their uneasy situation lay in the fact that they were subject to the authority of pagans totally ignorant of everything that had to do with what they treasured most, namely their religion. Whoever led them had the job of seeing that they were safeguarded from the twin evils of oppression and heathenism and of keeping their religion strong and their life undefiled, despite the Romans and their power. To him it fell to keep this fire and water in constant proximity, co-existing precariously. The Jews were minded to think that Caiaphas alone had the competence to achieve what they desired, if achieved it could be. There was, however, an envious element that had only ill to say of him, declaring that he would never govern Israel competently, considering how recalcitrant they were and difficult to lead. Their reason was that Caiaphas did not believe in brute force. Compelling people, even in their own interest, was not his way. He used to remark that if force won victories on behalf of truth they would only be the victories of force and not of truth. Force, by its very nature runs to excess and is soon found winning victories for what is false. He saw that if there was a clash between truth and falsehood and truth was worsted, human conscience and the course of history together would reform the evil, whereas if truth enlisted force and thereby triumphed but remained subordinate to force the net result would be the same as when it was still subordinate to falsehood. Since he was known for such principles, it was thought by some of his people that Caiaphas would never succeed in ruling so restive a nation as the Jews. Nor would he succeed, they thought, in handling the Romans, who believed in nothing else but force and never understood any argument he put to them. Nevertheless, his partisans were well aware that any forcible opposition to the Romans was a doomed and hopeless enterprise from the start. Tyranny would have to be resisted by other means. Jewry could have produced no more skilful adept of this art of passive non-violence than this very high priest.

Another group found fault with him on the ground that he had no real appetite for power. He approached authority as an ascetic might approach pleasure, perturbed that matters of life and death and people's destiny should depend on his word, a word that he might give without adequate reflection and thought. These critics held that the power he had undertaken was the very thing that disturbed and troubled his conscience. The only thing for him to do was to remain a scholar-philosopher and leave matters of state to those who could discharge them without distress of conscience. In point of fact those who take up high office fall into two groups. There are those who strive for it wholeheartedly and take any course whether fair or foul that gets them there. By contrast there are those whom their people set in authority because they trust them. Caiaphas was among the second. He was not the type to shrink from a leadership he disliked. Aware that there are plenty with the lust for power, he reasoned that at all events he would be less injurious than they, with an aloofness from harsh tyranny and selfish ambition they would never have.

None were so uneasy as the politicians when they saw Caiaphas assuming responsibility in their own field. His attitude to politics and politicians was well known. They were, it seemed to him, completely incapable of transcending immediate facts and thus no initiative in reform could be hoped for from them. Indeed they looked upon reform as an impossibility. Politics, as seen by politicians, is the pursuit of the possible and since reform means attaining what appears impossible, the two can never be had together. Caiaphas had the habit of saying that politicians know less than anyone about the job they undertake and that their leaders go along with events while thinking they direct them. They consider themselves at the summit of things, so long as the appearance of power is maintained, but are in fact subservient to the common people. One of his maxims was that just as there is tension and sharp disparity between ethics and life, so there is between the things of God and the things of politics. He did not mean any essential incompatibility but the difficulty from which everything stems of translating the Divine commands into political practice. It is as stubborn as that of translating ethical principles into daily living.

Caiaphas had been in authority in Israel for some time and with considerable success. He had been able to adopt a moderate attitude towards the Romans. He was neither too assertive nor too deferential. In relations with his own people he was just and sincere and they recognised his integrity. Their faith in him led them to tolerate from him what they would not have accepted from any one else. To be in the people's good graces is one of the greatest factors in a ruler's success, though it is difficult of attainment and only few succeed. The secret of such good success is an absolute sincerity, free from subterfuge, pretension and self-interest. Caiaphas was one of those goodly rulers in whose justice, good government and complete integrity people believed. The life of Caiaphas had been by no means a bed of roses. But he saw the right and wrong clearly. His instinct for the right course seldom failed him and only rarely was his judgement at fault. He was guided by clear intellectual principles and by them he exercised an honest rule over people and affairs. One factor that greatly helped was the attitude of the Roman governor, who, despite the usual Roman egotism, valued high principle and, as far as one could, reared among Roman aristocracy, understood issues of conscience and of truth.

Things went prosperously and satisfactorily with Caiaphas until the new message came into being among the Jewish people. It was very perplexing to know what he ought to do both about the message and the preacher. Though careful not to publicise the fact, he was not a little taken privately with what the message contained. One of the features about the new prophet which agreeably surprised him was the fact that he adopted a similar policy to that of Caiaphas towards the Romans. For Caiaphas too held strongly that they should leave him in control of the religion of his people and their communal life, while they were free to take what tribute money they wished. But he reserved his highest commendation of the new teacher for the way in which he couched this policy, when he said, in words that Caiaphas for all his wit and wisdom could not have aspired to: 'Give what belongs to Caesar to Caesar and what belongs to God give to God.'

But it was when he heard of 'the Kingdom of Heaven' that admiration reached its peak. All his life long Caiaphas had been searching for a decisive solution to a moral problem for which he had found no answer in the ideas of prophets and philosophers of which he was aware. It was the question of the reward for passive or hidden virtues, or virtues that were both passive and hidden. Everybody knows that active virtues like generosity, courage, beneficence, have open reward in the esteem with which men and women reverence and love them, as well as in the reputation and self-respect that go with them. But hidden virtues, like patience, abstention from evil doing, compassion for the weak, fidelity and kindness to the poor: these have no open recompense unless they come to be known, and that does away with their virtuousness, and may even degrade them to the point of their being hypocritical favours. Passive virtues, like humility, long-suffering, the renunciation of evil when there is advantage to be had in doing it, and the loyalty that refrains from evildoing even when prudence or self-indulgence or the avoidance of hardship or visions of success make evil inviting: these, being virtues of resistance, are often more difficult to achieve and sterner to maintain than the positive virtues which get the limelight and the acclaim. Caiaphas often reflected on the fact that such virtues characterised poor and ignorant and simple souls. To contemplate such souls and their quiet inner heroism filled his heart with admiration. He even noted in the lives of prostitutes and drunkards a courageous capacity to suffer, a sacrificial heroism and the virtue of patience. He would have liked to have been able to discover a reward for them. For it was unjust to have an ethical assessment that was partial to one class of people at the expense of others. He was not satisfied with the current answer that the reward of these virtues was an inward feeling of being right. That, it seemed to him, was an inadequate reward. If there was nothing more than that, most people, surely, would find it hard to keep a life-long grip on these virtues without despair and weariness.

He was led ultimately to a solution that pleased him. Human nature is an indivisible whole, an interdependent unity. Every worthy trait, however hidden, constitutes a stone in the building of the personality. Though its quality may be concealed, its effect is not lost. Those who think their sacrifices go for nothing, that their patience under distress is unrecognised, or that self-restraint on their part, whereby they forfeit great advantage, remains unnoted as if it were all the same thing to resist the allurements of evil and never to have faced them – all these people, each and all of them, should keep in mind that their deeds shape a worthy personality. If deeds in detail be unknown to society, personality none can mistake. Let them realise that their virtues and sacrifices are not in vain. Let them persevere in their pattern of life. There is reward enough in the stamp of personality by which they become known.

Caiaphas came to see, however, that the new prophet solved this whole problem in a finer and more impressive way. He created the kingdom of heaven concept as the reward of these hidden passive virtues. He declared it open to the poor and simple, to the ignorant and sinful. By so doing he restored to them their self-respect and gave them back their sense of being men and women, and recompensed them with good commensurate with their virtues. As Caiaphas saw it this was a remarkable solution, achieving a quality of justice which such people had hitherto been denied.

He was not unduly surprised at the attacks the initiator of the new message made upon the Pharisees. Caiaphas lost little love on them and paid them scant attention. He was of the opinion, though, that the open show of worship and of piety kept their claims before people's notice. If the worshipper was in fact a hypocrite, God would deny him any advantage from his worship and his pious show. But open performance served none the less to foster the practice of religion lest people should forget. So it might be a means of evoking from many a worship that was true and sincere.

Caiaphas was utterly opposed to the verdict of the new teacher relating to the woman whom the populace had sought to stone. He declared that, however noble and lofty might be the sentiments behind the ruling the Lord Christ[7] had given, it nevertheless sharply attacked a plain commandment of God and exegetically was quite unjustified. If people with perverse intentions were to invoke the precedent there would be no telling to what lengths they might not go in contravening religion and interpreting its laws. Caiaphas also set little store by the new prophet's miracles, reserving his admiration for the miracle of the lofty principles he taught and for his impressive solution of ethical problems which none before him had succeeded in solving so remarkably.

It was Caiaphas' conviction that nobody really understood the new preaching in its full range and import, except himself and the preacher. From the ethical point of view he could readily congratulate him on his achievement. But he was convinced it would never be any good in changing people's lives and characters. The new prophet, he told himself, would never be successful in reform of the human situation, despite the nobility of his principles and the depth of his thought. He had perhaps clarified what had to do with the individual human conscience, but was totally incapable of generating any conscience in communities. He seemed to be assuming that society would be alright if the individuals within it were right. The error was a familiar one. It was imperative to create in society a conscience that would forbid evil doing and to do so by direction of conscience alone without bringing compulsion to bear. For otherwise evil would persist among us, though every single one of us individually repudiated it.

Another of his observations about the new prophet was that he apparently wanted to set conscience above religious practice. But religious people would destroy him before the conscientious came to his rescue. He wanted to raise insignificant people to the same level as their superiors. But the latter would destroy him before those whose status he wanted to raise came to his rescue. He wanted love for humanity to take precedence over pride of nation and race. Nationalism, however, would destroy him before humanitarianism could deliver him. He had not harmed a single individual in Jewry, nor would a single Jew ever do him harm. But he was injuring Jewry as a corporate entity, and as a community they would have their revenge on him, even though every man jack of them hated to take personal revenge on him. Moreover, he said he was a prophet while his followers say that he is a God. Is he not in fact failing out of weakness? And when was weakness ever one of the attributes of God save according to him and his followers?[8] 'It will soon be clear to him that a mere man such as I am is more competent than he to bring about reform, prompted though he be by the Holy Spirit. Otherwise he should realise that reform is most likely to succeed when it keeps close to actuality. Sweeping reform action that is far out of touch with where people are has no hope of success. The true reformer is the one who begins gradually from where people really are. The new prophet should be aware that time is a major factor in all worthy change. Neither prophets nor gods can afford to neglect it. The message that could be good for humanity thousands of years hence becomes a veritable calamity if it is put into action before their souls have been prepared for it. Though he may be purer souled than I, with a finer conscience and a nobler character, I have it over him in action. I confer a larger benefit upon the human race.'

Thus when alone with himself did Caiaphas reflect, turning over quietly in his mind what related to the new religion and its inaugurator. He had no need for violent debate about the matter. But the whole of Israel was now agitatedly demanding the blood of the new prophet, having determined on a verdict of crucifixion against him. Caiaphas realised that the question had thus become a desperate affair that admitted of no mere philosophical discussion. It was now his duty to approve what they had decided the day before if it was right and to oppose them if they had reached a false decision.

Never in his life had Caiaphas known himself be so perplexed as he was now over this verdict which his nation had come to after careful debate and prolonged argument. Previously he had gone on the assumption that truth was a fairly obvious matter and that nothing was easier for honest minded folk than to see where it led and follow it. Today, however, it seemed to him that neither his sincerity, nor reason, nor wisdom could really avail him. The business weighed on him. He no longer knew what was right. It pained him that the pagan Roman governor, despite his coarse stamp of nature, had nevertheless so keen a mind and so sensitive a temper. Had he not remarked when the Jewish crowd demanded that he rid them of the new heretic for the sake of truth: 'Truth? what is truth?' Caiaphas regretted that he had not coined the phrase. He would like to have said that to his people before matters had reached such a pitch. Perhaps then they would have been rightly guided.

That night Caiaphas had passed sleeplessly, turning the thing over in his mind from every angle. His troubled thoughts fluctuated in a quite illogical and unaccountable fashion. At one time he was uplifted by noble aspirations and at another cast into the deepest gloom. He strove to discover some basic principle by which to reconcile his duty to conscience and his duty to politics, but without avail. He wrestled to bring either one or the other into dominance but without success. His thoughts were tormented by recollections from the depths of his past history, from events of his youth. He had no idea that these could still influence him now that he was well on in years. It was an interminably long night. In spite of himself he reviewed his entire life, mental and spiritual, as well as things that had no bearing on the issue that engrossed him. He had known nothing like it before.

In the agitation of his mind he began talking to himself:

'Why has this man brought his preaching particularly to us in Jewry who are all moral and religious people, the most tenacious of all people on earth about the commandments of God? Why is he concerned to purify our conscience, when we have the purest of any people in the world? Would it not be more fitting for him to go to Rome and preach his message there, where they are ignorant and pagan evil doers? Why doesn't he attempt to guide Rome's sinful oppressors? None could be in greater need of his wisdom. If he succeeded there he would be conferring an immense benefit on humanity. For Rome is the mistress of the world. In her hand is might and dominion. Even if his doctrine were to make headway among the people of Israel, no other nation would profit from it. I admire what he proclaims enormously. But I don't want his religion established here among us. In our present emergency what we need most of all is quietness, inner cohesion and unity. I am concerned lest what he says will provoke disruption and division in our ranks. Beyond that I do not care whether he is exalted to heaven, exiled to the end of the earth, or crucified – if God has willed he die a violent death. If that befalls him it will be by Divine decree and there's no reversing that. God knows more of the unknown than we.

'Perhaps this point is the beginning of the light which I must follow to be right. So I'll begin where I want to end. I do not desire his continuance in our midst on any condition. If crucifixion is the one way of getting him hence, then crucifixion let it be. And his crucifixion will be right. Also it will be my duty to sustain the judgement we reached against him yesterday in the hall of meeting.

'Yet how can such reasoning be right? The charges made against him do not represent what I think and yet it is my duty to uphold them. They charged him with falsehood and he is innocent of every accusation they made. Yet how can I acquit him of wrongdoing and yet agree to the sentence of death? If his innocence is publicly acknowledged it follows he must stay in our midst. Yet this in my view would be wrong. So then I am between two opinions over him. Either I have to get rid of him by the only way there is, that is, by charging him with wrong and deception in pursuit of an end I consider right. Or else to affirm his innocence and have him continue among us propagating his gospel, which is an evil I can not stomach. Yet if I accuse him of falsehood I shall myself have committed the very thing for which I have reproached the foulest and most ignorant in the scum of politics. Is it befitting for me to pursue evil means to attain a good end? Have I not spent my whole life telling people that the greatest evil is to suppose that the good end justifies the evil means? Evil means can never lead to good ends, absolutely never, except in idle fancy or for a brief time. In the end evil overcomes.

'Furthermore, my sense of justice, which is what I treasure most, will not let me pass over the unjust indictment against him. They have actually made their indictment out of the very finest principles in his gospel. They have accused him of calling men and women to trustfulness, righteousness and the love of their enemies, alleging that these things will be destructive of the virtues of the Jewish people and their way of life. They have charged him with sorcery, though he is no sorcerer. They have accused him also of preaching contrary to the book of God, which they allege to be unbelief on his part. Actually he has gone one step further than Moses went in the sacred law. I see no unbelief in that. Rather it is the law of God in its forward movement. In any case the whole accusation is the work of that ambitious prosecutor who wants to get to the top quickly, though his path be through sin and hatred. There's wrongdoing in his heredity: isn't his the family that denied me one of their daughters as a bride when I was young, because they despised my status? Their prime objective is to get him where I am.'

His ruminations at this point brought a blush of shame and distress to his face as if he had been taken unawares thinking unseemly thoughts he never should have harboured. Then he fell once more into soliloquy:

'But all this has nothing to do with my repudiation of his position of yesterday. He made a mistake I've no desire to fall into in his processes of thought, a mistake arising from his initial premiss that the man is a criminal. From this *parti pris* he began to search out where his view might lead. Most people fall into the same mistake. There are very few who gather all the factors together first before formulating their point of view. Most people take up a point of view and then look around for reasons. I used to think I had been emancipated from this years ago. Now today I find myself doing the very thing I know to be wrong. Did I not postulate at the outset that the man must be eliminated from our midst? Now, after my decision is taken, here I am seeking reasons and my mind is made up. Can I now deliver him when I have already fully persuaded the people that he is a menace to them? I am very much afraid that it will be impossible to rescue him today. I should have prohibited them from going on with the prosecution. What deterred me from doing so was simply that people would draw their own conclusions about me, that they would accuse me of being afraid of him, or of unbelief the same as they accused him. Had I resisted them, I would have been put out of office and he would not have been saved. If I resist them they will put me out of office. If I submit to their agreed verdict their purpose in his case will go through. In neither event can I save him. And if I were able to do so, he would remain among us, his cause all the more tremendous, which is not what I fancy at all. The whole perplexity in the matter goes back to the fact that his presence is a menace. And since he is innocent, what way is there to be rid of him other than injustice? Is he not a master of miracles? Let what will happen happen. If God has willed that he be slain then what business have we with rescuing him? If God wills that he be saved it is no business of mine to find the way. It doesn't need a strong faith to see that. I would never have thought, though, that I would have reached such a feeble position on any issue. But when I consult my reason I find no answering guidance.'

The morning came, with Caiaphas wearied and heavy hearted. He set out for the hall of meeting not knowing what he ought to do. His final idea was to let events take their own course. What power had he anyway to direct them in the way he wanted? He resolved to take up a position of neutrality. He would adopt whatever conclusion was agreed on by the learned leaders of his people and the masters of thought. Their reckoning and his was in the hand of God.

He no longer had any confidence in himself nor in human counsels, though he had believed strongly in the latter as a means of developing a conscience in the community. Society lacking a conscience of its own chooses individual persons to take common counsel in the hope that these individuals will act in the name of society with due regard to conscience. So he had thought: but now all assurance about truth and justice, religion and dogma, had left him. Had these availed now to guide him in the business about which he was so distraught? He had come to the conclusion that the guidance religion could afford was only of a general kind, incapable of application to specific situations. He felt utterly bankrupt: he was that day the most impotent of men. At the moment of crisis he was no better than the most ignorant and worthless of his people.

Had he been able then to set eyes on the one condemned to crucifixion, he would have seen a man serenely at peace within himself, untroubled by doubt or indecision. He would have realised too that the secret of the contrast was that the new prophet spoke out of firm convictions without a care for the reactions his message might arouse. All that mattered was that it was true. His teaching had to do wholly with conscience and he cared nothing about popular politics, holding only to the spirit and to conscience. The frailty of human nature, prone to turn the good into evil and to confuse the true and the false, had not entered into his calculations. He listened only to conscience, and he who finds his guidance there and nowhere else will never go astray.

# The Hall of Meeting

A great crowd had gathered in front of the hall of meeting and they were crying at the tops of their voices: Kill him! crucify him! burn him! He's a dangerous sorcerer. Kill his followers, they are traitors and apostates! Caiaphas entered the place of assembly dejected and oppressed. He greeted those present in a listless, half-hearted kind of way, as his eye wandered round the company. He noted the public prosecutor, the very sight of whom was enough to bring the blood to his cheeks, as he murmured to himself: 'If he gets up today and repeats what he said yesterday I will challenge and refute him. I'll give the lie to his words and deride his ideas and let the chips fall where they will.' Like the rest, he assumed that this youth would be the first to take the floor, returning to the charge with the same brilliance and force of persuasion, and carrying his audience with him in a firm adherence to their point of view. But he remained in his seat in silence. Though people looked in his direction, he had no mind, in his confusion, to open the debate.

The first to speak was a venerable scribe who began by saying: 'Soon I will be going to meet my Maker: I do not want to meet Him either as a deceiver or as one deceived. Yesterday you listened to me at great length. You were told my opinion was that it is unlawful to preach any law as higher than the law given from heaven to Moses. For that would imply that we are improving on God's mistakes, the very idea of which is rank blasphemy. Or it would imply that after God had laid down His law, it came to Him to change it, as if His knowledge had been faulty. Both implications are a denial of the faith. They are intolerable to anyone who belongs to the faith of Israel.

'What I actually said, however, was something rather different. I do not deny the high idealism in this man's teaching. What I hold against him is that he makes it by his own authority an integral part of religion. He wants to oblige all to follow it as revelation sent down from heaven. What I feel is that it should be taken as no more than a guiding light good to be followed by anyone who feels able freely to do so. But whoever is unable to do so shall not be put in the wrong thereby, nor be regarded as contravening religion. If the matter is left to rest there, it will not in any way affect the faith, either closely or remotely. Moreover, the only reason impelling me to this position is my apprehension for our religion. It is incumbent upon us jealously to safeguard its inviolability and its sanctity, its commandments and prohibitions. One of the dangers for religion is when it comes to be regarded in the popular mind as arduous in its commandments, so that they are widely disobeyed, or as having exacting prohibitions that involve much privation and give little immunity from trouble. My experience of human nature has taught me that anyone who goes counter to religious obligations when they are difficult readily contravenes them when they are simple. If the injunctions of faith become so lofty that only the few can attain them, the gulf between religion and life widens and this of course weakens its effect on social improvement. The capacity of religion to bring about reform derives from the respect in which it is held. One of the situations that undermines religious reverence is for people to venture on obedience and then find themselves inadequate to follow through its teachings.

'Men of religion and learning take up contrasted positions on this issue. One group considers that religion only benefits humankind when it is feasible and operative. They liken humanity to a caravan which must proceed at a speed within the capacity of the slowest. As long as this condition is fulfilled its progress will at least be steady and will not run into trouble or come to grief. But if it is obliged to advance at the pace of the strongest, the resulting strain will make everybody restive and it will not cover the ground or even keep going. This point of view holds that God knows best what suits us. What He has given to us in revelation has to be implicitly followed without addition or omission. Jewry belongs to this first school of thought, certainly I do and for this view of the matter I invite your approval.

'However, there is another group, consisting of eminently devout persons, who hold that religion should be the sum of the highest ideals known, irrespective of whether we are able to bring our lives into line with all their teachings. Religion must be constant, sound, high-principled and consistent. If it is measured by what befits a particular people at a particular time, it will be endangered by natural progress. The lapse of time, the advance of humanity and the expansion of science and reason may overtake it. Social systems develop and popular attitudes towards social justice reach a higher level beyond present day standards. Then religion might find itself, and its dicta, inferior to ordinary, man-made laws and precepts. Such a situation would constitute the greatest possible danger to religion as a whole.

'I believe that the new prophet holds this second point of view. He has set his religion unsurpassed standards of moral law and is unconcerned about its practicability in popular life. I do not share this attitude. But at the same time I do not claim that I am immune from error. Nor do I say that his message amounts to blasphemy. It may be that my idea is mistaken. The character of Jewish religion on which I have just commented may be a factor hindering its expansion in the world. It may also be that the very remoteness of the new religion from daily life, as we know it, is one factor in its greatness and its growth. These matters all depend on knowing hidden mysteries of which I claim no knowledge. But as far as my reason takes me, it seems to me that religion is in danger when high idealism becomes an integral part of it. When its commands and prohibitions become so lofty that only a very small select group can cope with them, people become prone to neglect it altogether in respect of what is easy as well as in what is arduous.'

The audience listened to the faltering old doctor of the law alleging that they had misconstrued his views, but were unable to follow what he said. However, it had critical implications for what had been said in the prosecution speech and these, the listeners thought, the speaker of yesterday would not allow to pass unchallenged. So when the eminent lawyer had had his say, they craned their necks expectantly in the direction of the prosecutor, and awaited his retort. But he seemed crestfallen and had not a word to say, which for him was astonishing.

Whereupon the mufti got up and said that an error had somehow crept into the interpretation of his remark about the miracles. He had not asserted that they were false, nor did he decry the good things that had been accomplished at his hands. He then proceeded to expound his complicated point of view about the miracles. Though the audience did not understand much of what he said, they gathered that on the whole the speaker had no basic quarrel with the miracle-worker.

'People have not kept a proper balance in discussing these supernatural works. We in Jewry are generally immoderate in what we say. The very eloquence of our language tempts us to generalities and sweeping statements. We say that the flood covered the earth when what we mean is that it merely covered our village. We talk about the world being thrown into darkness when we mean simply that darkness enveloped us. Similar exaggeration is very evident in what people say about the miracles. If it were stripped of all this hyperbole we could take the residue as being true and unadulterated.'[9]

Pursuing his theme he declared:

'It is useless to deny the occurrence of events to which the word "supernatural" is applied. Undoubtedly they have happened. It is pointless to seek an explanation of their occurrence that would pass them off as delusory or deceptive. There is in fact nothing illusory or fraudulent about them. But in my view they are events that do not go outside the natural order. It is the time and manner in which they occur, together with the results to which they give rise, that makes them seem more than ordinary. Let me offer an example to explain what I mean. Imagine a man actively meditating murder as an act of revenge. During a raging storm he is stricken by a thunderbolt and perishes at that very juncture. Such things are familiar enough contingencies and befall the innocent too. It may even happen to a man engaged sincerely in prayer to God. Now the fact that it eventuates at that very moment and destroys the evildoer makes it a miracle for those who know him to be such, whereas those unaware of this fact would not consider a man's death because of a thunderbolt to be a miracle.

'Look at the miracles performed by this new teacher. He feeds thousands of people with a few loaves, turns water into wine, raises the dead and restores lots of sick folk. No one claims that he fed thousands of wild horses or hungry lions with a few loaves. Nobody has said that he prayed for them and they felt satisfied. What actually happened was that he fed a company of believers with a little food. Being convinced believers in him, their faith made them satisfied with this little. Likewise the story of the water into wine. He gave the people water and they felt the taste and effect of wine. The real miracle lay in his power to influence people and the intensity of their faith in him. When he raised the dead there was no transcendance of the natural order. He did not call Lazarus back to life for ever; nor did he raise all the dead. His restoring the sick was doubtless a blessing and a mercy: we have no ground for repudiating him on that score. Miracles are only false when they break a fundamental natural law. If we were to see him commanding a stone to rise in the air and it were to do so, I would certainly regard him as a sorcerer who was deceiving us. When, however, miracles have to do with psychological matters, where faith and belief are operative, there is no reason for defaming him.'

He sensed that the audience was having a hard time following this bewildering discussion, so he terminated it by saying:

'Whether these views of mine about the miraculous are true or false, one thing cannot be questioned. All the miracles he has performed have been for the good of others. We are not aware of any of our people he has harmed by them nor of any enemy of his on whom he has used them for revenge. What you have heard today about his inflicting harm on an innocent merchant and blacksmith, with no guilt to their names, is fatuous talk that ill becomes you, though the vulgar throng may believe it. Had he in his heart any desire for vengeance against any of his countrymen, he would surely have avenged himself on us who sentenced him to death.'

Many of those present were no longer heeding what he said. They took him to be defending the miracle-worker and to hold the view that these doings did not amount to an apostacy worthy of punishment by death. In fact all his marvellous works were a benediction of goodness.

Caiaphas was astounded to see that his people listened tolerantly to such words of vindication of the teacher. Apparently they had changed their minds, as he had himself, about their day's work yesterday. His amazement knew no bounds when another speaker took the floor and said:

'We accused them yesterday of betraying their nation. It is a foul and dastardly charge. Love for one's motherland is a virtue none will deny. But it is not the ultimate virtue of virtues. Patriotism is one of the stages of social progress. The individual starts out by loving himself alone. Such self-love is useful to him and preserves him from harm. Later it becomes clear to him that love and concern for his family lead to still greater benefit. They also make a better defence against trouble than isolated individual action. In this way there develops in his mind the sense of self-sacrifice in the service of his family. Then it becomes clear that his love for his tribe or his city holds for him greater potentialities of advantage and protection than he can achieve of himself if he limits his efforts to his own family. He comes to realise that evil befalling his tribe or city involves him also individually in loss he cannot of himself remedy. Then it becomes natural he should subordinate both self and family to the interests of tribe or city.

'There follows the discovery that a vigilant patriotism offers greater advantages and gives better defence against ill fortune than tribe or city are capable of. And again it is evident that evil befalling a nation afflicts the individual too. It may even deny him what he values most. Though he may be in no way responsible for bringing about what is so disastrous to his nation, he nevertheless willingly admits the propriety of self-sacrifice in order to preserve it. Thus he sets the nation above himself, his family and his tribe.

'But this is not the end of the story. The day must come when the social order reaches a point at which people are persuaded that to love and safeguard humanity as a whole is a more appropriate thing for any nation that mere patriotism. The entire world will be a unity in which love of humanity will bring to pass for every nation benefits such as no restrictive nationalism could procure. When that happens men and women will begin to think as one humanity. We will see them setting the service of humanity above the service of the nation. Nor will that constitute any treachery to the nation. Rather it will spell the truest security and the fullest prosperity. It may be that this teacher is the first to arrive at this ultimate of moral progress. However, let me not conceal from you that I am not easy in my mind about trying to bring our people of Israel to this persuasion, setting humanitarian principles above nationalism, while we continue in these present tribulations, downtrodden and humiliated in our own country. This may be feeble on my part. The fact is that I understand these principles that set humanity over nation well enough in my mind, but I find I do not believe them wholeheartedly. Perhaps it is due to weakness in my belief, and maybe I considered there was no urgency in applying them in our time even had I believed in them as fervently as he does.'

He gave them an example to clarify his meaning:

'Love of one's nation becomes a man morally, just as an anklet ring is a becoming adornment for a woman. Some woman because of poverty may have no anklet and in the same way, through moral poverty a man may be completely lacking in patriotic feeling. Yet a prosperous woman, too, may have no anklet because she regards them as unbefitting. So too a man may abandon his patriotism on the ground that he is too progressive for such partial virtues and lesser loyalties. But this could only be the case when a woman had actually acquired a better and worthier adornment than an anklet. Similarly with the erstwhile patriot who must have come by greater and finer virtues than patriotism – since it would be improper for anybody not to have either the one or the other. Only humanitarian love can properly supersede nationalism, being a form of moral progress that is more worthy. So it is quite invalid for us to regard such humanitarianism as a shame or a fault in this teacher whom we have condemned for treachery. Regarding himself as the trustee of all humanity, he is much too wide in his sympathies to think of himself merely as a nationalist.'

These remarks fell like a thunderbolt upon an audience that had accepted the belief that the new messenger was a traitor. Yet no one made a move to break the ensuing silence. Caiaphas concluded that the prosecution had collapsed and that they would rescind the verdict they had taken the day before. His surprise and perplexity intensified and he felt growing doubt about everything. He decided to let events take their own course without attempting to direct them. Already they were tending the way that pleased him and he was mightily glad.

Voices outside the meeting hall, however, grew louder, insisting on the death of the man and his followers. The ground of these demands was that the learned leaders had already so decreed. Were not they the wise and knowing people, who could not agree on an error? Yet these very men were there and then realising that they were greatly in the wrong. They dreaded going out to the people and acknowledging the fact, with indication of their repentance. Perhaps some of them, as individuals, would have been capable of such courageous action. But it was completely inconceivable for them to do so as a body. Communities as such are always more capable of behaving rashly than of seeing reason, of contriving to survive even at the price of falsehood than of turning back to the truth.

While they were in this state of indecision some of the men of property, merchants and artisans, influential people of the world, entered the hall intending to offer them their congratulations on the soundness of their verdict. When they discovered instead this hesitancy and doubt, they were angered and exclaimed:

'What's the idea? Do you suppose you can go back on your mind having made it up and announced it openly? People have accepted it as right. Do you imagine they will tolerate being fooled in this way? Your verdict has set in motion a flood of wrath which nobody can now hold back. Moreover, what would the Romans say, were you to go to them today reversing what you decided earlier? Do you think they will take you seriously? Or give you another answer tomorrow? The people are in an ugly rebellious mood. They will never be quietened unless this man is crucified today.'

The people rushed into the hall crying out: 'Crucify them, burn them all: they must all be crucified together, he and they.' The disorder mounted. The leaders of opinion were overborne and deprived of their proper role. They dispersed without having altered their decision in any way. The throngs made their way to the palace of the Roman governor to demand the blood of the teacher and his disciples. Yet there was not one among them who knew any evil about him, none who sought his death out of belief or personal conviction. Thus was accomplished the greatest of the crimes of history, the crime of the condemnation of Christ to crucifixion as one who had denied God, without anybody in Jerusalem knowing who it was who wanted his death nor upon whom the guilt of this foul deed really fell.

The fact was that no one in Jewry knew assuredly anything evil against the community of the preaching. They were merely closing ranks behind reports of their evil doings. It may well be that the first to allege evil of them only had an idea without realising where it would end, and never intended such a climax. It was just like what happens with a flock of sheep when the first goes through a gate or takes to a path. They all follow precipitately and their course gets set so that there is no changing it. The first sheep would be unable to turn them about even if he so desired.

Thus was Christ condemned to die on a cross for having denied God! Can anyone thereafter feel the slightest confidence in human wisdom?

From the point of view of the human involvement, the crime was accomplished when Christ was condemned to death. The fact that God raised him to Himself in no way mitigates the iniquity of what was done.

The wrong was only carried through by dint of being parcelled out among a large number of people, so that no single individual had any longer to think of himself as personally responsible.

How grievously did humanity go astray in this course of action, to come to such a pitch of misguidedness. The same path opens itself continually before the children of Adam and they continue to go far down it in evil doing. They will go on doing so, until faith in conscience leads them into the way of true guidance. There is no safeguard for them from perverted choices save in such a faith.

# 4. With the Disciples

# Woman of Magdal

The town of Magdal, one of the provincial towns of Palestine, had never in all its history had any other dominant family. Sometimes the population submitted contentedly to these masters and at other times heartily detested them. Some were kindly, while others were brutal tyrants: some brought a zeal for reform, others the bane of corruption. One result of this long ascendancy was to generate in the men of the ruling family a highly aristocratic temper, in senses both fair and foul. Aristocratic attitudes are always brought into being that way. It happens in tiny villages and likewise in mighty cities, though the manifestations vary.

The head of the family at the time of this action was a good and upright man whose only care was that peace might prevail in his little kingdom and that his people should enjoy a happy and quiet existence. With his wealth he treated them beneficently and their security he made a matter of his personal honour. Public affairs went well while he himself pursued his private life pleasantly enough. His daughter was his greatest treasure and the pride of his wife's heart. They vied with one another in pampering her and never wearied doing so. She grew up the delight of their lives and no whim of hers was ever refused. When she ripened into her full beauty her feminine charm was perfect. Her gracefulness was striking, even ravishing. Yet somehow her presence overawed men rather than drew them to her in attraction. It was not long before she became the belle of the town and every eligible youth sought her for his wife. Her family wanted her to make her own match and choose her husband. But she was intensely proud, indeed unbearably egotistical. She looked on everyone with a habitual disdain and a fastidious eye. Her arrogance and vanity led her to think that no youth in the town was a proper match for her. She spurned them all.

One of them accordingly had the idea of banding together some young bloods of his age to bring her pride into ridicule. This led him into both doing and saying unseemly things, which aroused her brother's anger. He considered it his duty to protect her and her family from the follies of these pranksters. The men of the town were divided, one part siding with the brother the other part with the prankster. Finally they fell to battling with sticks. When the quarrel intensified they used knives and daggers. The conflicts of the town's youth developed into a fully fledged rebellion against the age-long authority of the ruling family. Several were killed in the battle, including the girl's brother. The quiet, peaceful community was plunged into grief. Families brooded in their homes broken-hearted over the loss of children, husband, a brother or some friend. Both the stupid origins and the sudden onset of the tragedy only deepened the gloom.

The girl, too, with the rest of the community, was grief-stricken about events and she had the intolerable burden of having been the ultimate cause of them. Her pride and vanity had been the source of everything. Remorse and sorrow raged within her. She was shunned and ostracized by the townsfolk who, with no angry shows of detestation, just let her severely alone. It pained her so that she wearied of life and no one befriended her or consoled her. No one pleaded any palliative that might have lessened the anguish she suffered over what she had brought upon her people. Her despair was complete when she realised that even her mother had turned against her. Only her father remained any solace to her and even his kindliness was not a little forced and guarded. Later her mother relented somewhat out of a sense that it was her duty to deal gently with her daughter. But she faced the duty with no warmth of conviction. This forced kindliness was a sorer trial to her tormented spirit than any outright hatred and hostility.

One day she realised that she was coming inevitably to a point where her distress could well drive her mad, if she stayed any longer in the town. She resolved to take her journey to Jerusalem, where, as generally in teeming cities, nobody knew anything about their neighbours. She made out she wanted to make a pilgrimage to the temple, seeking forgiveness. When her mother learned of her desire she did not oppose it. So the hapless girl left the town, with none to bid her farewell and none to regret her departure. When she had left Magdal behind her, she could almost hear the local folk breathing deep sighs of relief at the news of her exit from their midst.

Despair and sorrow of heart made her very irresolute as she entered Jerusalem. She could not think. Though she had adequate material resources for a long time, without having to worry, she had no notion what to do in the great city. Her burning desire was to expiate the sin of her pride. Only in utter self-abasement could there be atonement for pride. Then she would deliberately live among the dregs of society. There were plenty of women in the lower strata of the world far less guilty than she, whose sins were lighter than hers.

Some of the folk in the city took her for an unattached woman who did not know her own mind. There came across her one of those men who are all too numerous in great cities, who delight in pestering a solitary woman and surround her with occasions of temptation. He engaged her in conversation and made amorous advances, pursuing his suit with some vehemence and conjuring up for her a life of pleasure and indulgence such as she might readily enjoy in certain houses known to him and frequented only by a small choice group of the better class. She rewarded his pains and his presumption in broaching to her such a proposal with kicks and blows. Yet from two points of view the suggestion attracted her. It would enable her to find the lowest depth of humiliating degradation which would expiate her offences. It would also afford men what men had fought each other for – the enjoyment of her body. They would have of her what they desired: it would be another form of expiation, befitting the kind of crime she had been guilty of when she had earlier denied men such things and they had slain each other for lack of them.

So she entered a certain house in Jerusalem, though she had

nothing in common with its inmates, who did not consider her one of their sort. She lacked both their characteristics and their vulgar manners. So they did not register any particular enthusiasm, or jealousy or hatred at her presence. They concluded there was something mysterious somewhere and they accepted her with the thought that her beauty and her singular charm would soon take her beyond their kind of place.

It was not long before she adopted a surprising and unusual regimen with her women colleagues and male visitors, a regimen quite out of keeping with the traditional practices of the life she had newly taken up. She would not sit long with the men nor talk with them much. She would have nothing to do with a man who did not kiss her hand with deference and respect. Any who had been some time with her she helped on their way with banter and scorn, speeding them along with a painful kick in the pants as she thrust them through the door. The occupants of the house considered such behaviour detrimental to their trade. But because of her great beauty and force of character, none of them dared to criticize her. Though depraved themselves, they admired this pride and superiority in her.

The only result was to increase the flow of clients to her and their slavish submissiveness to her only deepened her contempt for them. It became clear to her that this low life was in fact far from diminishing her pride. She had degraded herself but she had not expiated her sinfulness. Rather her vanity had intensified and become insufferable. One day an important Roman commander came to her and began kissing her hand, desiring her ardently. But she flared up angrily feeling that he was not deferential and had omitted to admire her beauty. She sent him on his way with a vicious kick – she had no idea she could reproduce one so hefty. He came back at her with his hand on his sword, intent on wiping out the disgrace with her blood. She did not flinch and showed no fear, but turned on him to kick again. Awed at this, he regained his self-possession and made his way out. When the other women heard what had happened, they came in haste expecting to find her trembling with apprehension about what she had got into. But they found her composed and quite unperturbed. She had thought he would kill her in revenge for what she had done. Then there would truly be an atoning for her sin of pride of the sort she had striven for and failed to find. So deeply despairing had she come to be that she had taken to hoping for death as the expiation of her sins. She was bitterly angry that what she wished for still eluded her.

The days went by and there was no denying that she remained as arrogant as ever. Men continued to be passionately in love with her, despite the scorn and disgrace she continually meted out to then. Had she known that men would put up with her boastings and vanity she would have chosen a husband from the townsmen of Magdal. What repelled her had been that she had seen no one among them worthy of her respect and she had no idea they would tolerate her scornful attitudes towards them. She did not know that infatuation for physical beauty gives men a capacity for abasement that makes them bear the utmost humiliation.

Then one day there came to the house a Roman soldier in the prime of youth. He was unusually gentle and quiet, with a somewhat dreamy and delicate look. Immediately she saw him she felt a sense of tenderness or love such as she had not experienced before. She yearned to sit beside him and converse. But she restrained herself and left him to her colleagues who enthused over him amorously. They could not believe that he was really a soldier who would fight and do battle, for he was still very youthful. Their incredulity angered him. He began to retail to them stories about his bravery and valour and how he had vanquished his enemies and struck terror into their hearts. But they only laughed among themselves, being quite unimpressed by what he said. They were familiar enough with the boastful ways of soldiers and their wild claims about their feats of arms. The girl from Magdal, as she listened to his words, began to feel that they were somehow different from the usual yarns of soldiers. As she sat there she looked hard at him telling how he had struck a victim on the head a powerful blow and felled him as if he had been a lifeless lump. It seemed to her, though, that his expression told a different story of grief and distress over the deed he had committed. Perhaps it had been his first victim and so there was a mental image of him clearly in his mind, and it was evident that the recollection gave him no pleasure.

She came to him with a question:

'Did your victim cry out?'

'Of course not; he neither cried nor groaned. His corpse lay motionless.'

'Are you sure about what you say?'

'There is not the least doubt. A man doesn't cry out or groan when he's had a deliberate blow on the head that's carefully aimed, not a blow that somebody tries to land with haste and in stealth.'

'This is the sort of hollow prating we are quite familiar with from you soldiers. Is there a man among you deserves to be believed? Can't you for once tell me the truth about this, for it concerns me deeply?'

'Truly I assure you that the man I killed neither cried out nor uttered a groan.'

'I wish I could rely on your word.'

Then on a sudden impulse she left them. She seemed both exasperated and weary. No one understood her secret behind her interrogation. There had been evident grief and urgency in the questions she had put.

The fact of the matter was that from the time of her brother's death she had been obsessed with the thought of a voice, as of somebody crying out, which she heard in the silence of the night. It disquieted her no end. She believed it was the voice of her brother crying out as he fell. She had no doubt that at that moment he cursed her, she whose pride had been the cause of his death. So when she heard the soldier's words she fondly hoped that his was a truthful account. She might then find peace of heart and be reassured that her brother had not cried out when he was killed, and that the voice she had heard at night was simply one of the effects of the troubled state of mind she had known ceaselessly since that day. That night she did sleep peacefully without hearing the voice that had so disturbed her, or the cry of her brother pitilessly calling her and never forgiving her the sin that had occasioned his death. Such tranquillity was new to her: she had not known it since the day of the tragedy and she was overjoyed.

The youth returned the next day. He was afraid that perhaps she was angry with him, but was much relieved when she greeted him with a cheerful smile. He came up to her wistfully. But mockingly she said to him:

'This is the dashing hero who dazzled us with his heroism and with all he had to tell of it. But let me ask you: Are you confusing vainglory on your part for heroism, and your gratification for courage? A fine thing to prick your conscience when you declare that you killed a man of whom you knew nothing and who had done you no harm.'

'What's to reproach in that? I have a friend who says there's no harm to folk in one man's being killed or even in the murder of many men, so long as women beget more every day.'

She smiled at this idea which she took for a mere jest. It did not enter her head that there were people who really thought like that and proceeded to act accordingly.

'Do you share this notion of your friend's? I had thought you would have agreed with those who consider the killing of an innocent man, whom you do not know nor he you, a deed which human conscience can in no sense justify, whether it be killing in war or any other way. It's all the same.'

'You are one of those who talk incessantly about conscience and religion, faith and unfaith, sin, atheism and repentance. We talk only little and rarely about such things. Our conversation is mainly or wholly about discipline and bravery, prowess and force, triumph over hardship, the slaughter of the enemy and love of glory. By these we have mastered the world: you however don't even rule your own selves.'

She saw he was growing irritated with a question which interested him little. He only wanted to talk love with her, the love which had monopolised his thoughts since their meeting of yesterday. It came to her mind to thank him for her deliverance from the imagined accusations that disturbed her slumbers. But she held back, thinking she would give him no grounds for making love to her. She went on with the topic she had first broached.

'And did you feel, as a courageous hero who had exposed himself to certain danger, that you really ruled as your people any whom you would not have ruled had you been all along in Rome? Don't you see that you are in just the same position as you were before you risked death in war? You victorious conqueror, do you feel that you are ruling anybody who is above your sort, even among the people of this hapless country? Do you think you have become master over one of the rich and great men of this country? Only those Romans who are their equals rule over them. Do you think you have gained anything from this supremacy that at all justifies the dangers you have encountered and the sin of killing the innocent which you now carry? The conquering soldier only enjoys supremacy at the very hour of conquest when there is confusion everywhere. Then all goes back to where it was before and he has no more authority over anybody than he had at the outset.'

'Anyhow, those who die in war build up Rome's glory.'

'You mean the glory of ten or twenty people in Rome. And what is this glory? Is it that ridiculous procession in which Caesar rides with his captives dragged behind his chariot? For you it is the height of glory when kings and princes are in the midst of such slaves. Kings they once were in their own lands, but in captivity they are like any other slaves. But is this the glory you are boasting about?'

'You are harassing me to think and, as we see it, soldiers ought not to think. The soldier has no loyalty except to discipline and this takes over his conscience and his mind, making the man a docile instrument. This is his excuse if he becomes conscienceless.'

The girl saw that the young man was not particularly well endowed with intelligence and that the conversation was wearisome to him. This caused her some surprise for he had plenty of sensitive charm which made him entirely worthy of kindly treatment. She wanted to kiss him and was sure she could love him if she had him to herself. Somewhat alarmed at these sentiments, she blushed with embarrassment to think that a longing desire for a man had actually taken hold of her. She regarded her encounters with men day by day as something having to do merely with her body. It was all in the realm of animality. When she sensed her own soul reaching out in desire towards a particular man with whom she had no connection, it seemed to her utter lustfulness. She was ashamed of being enmeshed like that in sin. She had no such feelings, however, when it was purely a matter of the flesh between her and men.

As these thoughts went through her mind, she got up quickly and left him. But she glanced at him expressively as she did so and he understood that she would not be averse to see him return whenever he wanted.

He did return to her the next day. Without acknowledging her desire even to herself, she had been waiting for his coming. It was as if she despised her longing for him. When he arrived she kept to her room and left him to her companions, who gladly took him on with unseemly jests and voluptuous play and lewd talk. He began to regale them with titbits of Roman camp conversation – how the army revelled in one of their heroes who single-handed had killed five inhabitants of a distant village. When they were thus roused against him he killed the lot of them. So the name of Rome had struck terror into the hearts of all the population of the country. None would ever dare stand hence forward before a Roman, however weak or base a Roman he might be. 'The commander has hailed him as the ideal Roman soldier and orders us to retaliate so sternly and fiercely against those who resist us that men will be filled with terror when the name of Rome is mentioned. This is the only way for Romans to perpetuate their power wherever they spread their empire.' The conversation dragged on while the soldier waited hopefully for the appearance of his other friend. But she did not present herself and, weary of waiting, he asked after her. He got up with her comrades to go and find her. There was a bustle of noise as they did so, but when they entered her room, he and they fell silent. He went up to her and kissed her hand while they rehearsed to her how ardently he wanted her and how their conversation jaded him. As they made for the door she halted them and they all stayed, with a show of courtesy and politeness that was not usual with them. He was delighted that she seemed content and all the women were happy to see her welcoming them and abandoning her old habit of keeping aloof and alone. She began on a bantering note, remarking that his hands were stained with blood and that she had no liking for sessions with bloodshedding criminals, though she did not mean a word she said. Every feature of this gentle youth showed how far he was from being a murderer of the innocent and a habitual shedder of blood. She pretended she wanted to go out. Whereupon he took hold of her garment begging forgiveness and protesting that he would never again kill a man and never henceforward ignore his conscience. He wept in her arms and she could not but believe in his penitence. When he went out he was truly happy in another's happiness with him.

To believe had become for her an inescapable necessity. She was in dire need of this new love, coming thus into her life for the first time. For in it she would find escape from remorse and discover peace of mind, in coming to feel that her arrogance, if not altogether gone, was assuredly going. Its intensity had already much abated, to her great joy. For all her previous effort in deliberately degrading herself in the practice of prostitution had been of no avail. In the humiliation of her body there had come no humbling in her soul. Yet now when for the first time she had experienced a pure and guileless love, her soul had been sweetly humbled in the way she had dreamed of but never attained. It became clear to her that the pride which was her great sin could only be atoned for by the way of pure love. For it was that which had humbled and cleansed her. She was certain that if only she had loved at the outset she would never have fallen into her first sin, nor would she have fallen back on to her second sin, which she had thought would be her expiation for the first. This state of conscious love did not persist very long. The enjoyment of it was short-lived. She soon passed beyond this sweet and simple passion, this lovely dream, this happy serenity, into another love deeper, sharper, more pervasive and wider in its range of virtues. When she became aware of this larger love she knew that the first was no more than a drop in the ocean. She forgot it completely. When afterwards she met the youth again, though she did not repel him, she left him alone, as though she had no recollection of that day when her heart had yearned at the sight of him and of how her soul had learned purity because of him. She forgot it all, as thirst is forgotten when the thirsty traveller comes to a little spring and is joyously refreshed, but later finding the broad river forgets the tiny fountain and how good it was.

So it was that one day she sat at her window watching for the young man's visit when she still wrestled with her desire for him. At times she got the better of it but at others it was too strong for her. For an hour she would indulge her yearning for him and strive hard for hours to forget him. While she was in this state of mind a man of eminence in the community came in laughing derisively, clapping his hands as he exclaimed:

'Well! today I've seen a wonder the like of which was never heard before. I can only think that the hour is near if our fortunes continue in this way. Don't you know what happened in Jerusalem today? A common man, with no power, authority[10] or rank, and who has no pretensions to property or learning, rode into Jerusalem on a donkey, a wretched stumbling donkey, like enough to throw its rider and break its own neck. He entered the city accompanied by the riff-raff of Israel, some of whose garments still smelt heavily of fish — for most of them are fisher folk of his from Galilee — a mob of ignorant, feeble-minded and poverty-stricken wretches such as you hardly find the like of in Jerusalem. In this disgraceful fashion did this man enter our city, with an olive branch in his hand as a token of his call to peace. He preaches, too, that we should love each other and that there should be love too between God and us. His followers say that he is a prophet who performs miracles and heals the sick. It is even said that he raises the dead. And there are sundry other superstitions among those who believe in him. He calls to a new faith and a special religion of his own which sets the poor above the rich, the ignorant above the learned and the weak above the strong. I had thought the craziness of this message and the feeble capacities of its propagators were enough to ensure its being treated with ridicule and utter contempt. I am quite appalled to find how acceptably people take it and to see their confidence in him as they crowd around. Yet I cannot think that anyone can believe in him who has not abandoned all hope of success in life.'

The girl from Magdal began asking about the preacher of the new message, about his identity, his sermons and his followers. She discovered that this challenger of Jerusalem preached mutual love among all people and love between God and humanity. He proclaimed humility as the source of all virtues, the path of prosperity and the means to abiding happiness. She learned that he forgave trespasses and pardoned sins. The realisation came upon her that her salvation would be through this man, this teacher who left aside the rich and learned and healed men and women of their pride. Her face lit up at the very thought in her soul. She stood up in her room as a sign for those present to go. When they did so she slipped out of the house secretly and fled with only one thought in her mind. She was bareheaded and clad only in flimsy attire. She feared to lose time and be late for the hour of blessed deliverance, dreading that what she had set her heart on might elude her. She was in no state for a woman to be abroad on the streets but she was blindly unaware of all around her. She recked nothing of what might be said of her. All her wealth she had left behind: she hastened whither she might find this man. She had made up her mind that he would be her captain of salvation.

It was not a difficult matter to find him, for there was a great crowd gathered about him. Some onlookers merely wanted to be able to say they had seen him: others sought healing for their sicknesses and there were others who followed him out of real faith in him. She started to cut her way through into the middle of the throng. From her very appearance and garb anyone could tell that she was not a virtuous woman. People drew away from her and thus opened a way around her, a sort of corridor lined with disgusted glances and looks of scorn. Giving them no heed, she went steadily forward towards him, but was unable to see his face as he did not turn in her direction. Then it happened that some woman or other touched him and he knew that it was the touch of a believer. Although everybody was in fact thronging him he was only aware of them when this believing woman touched him. The touch of the believer is something only he discerns. At that point the teacher turned around to ask who it was who had touched him. As soon as she saw his face the fugitive girl was entranced at the sight of him. She knew that her hope of salvation would not this time be disappointed. With a shout she declared to him her faith, her conviction that in him was her deliverance. He gave a sign to her to follow him. Many were angered with him, as a prophet on whom men had set their hopes, for receiving such a one as her. When he knew of their disgust he said to them these impressive words: 'The wise shepherd concerns himself with the lost among his sheep and rejoices over it when it returns to him and leaves those that do not stray.' But many of the bystanders did not regard these sentiments as adequate to justify his tender dealings with the girl and his welcome to her when she was an obvious sinner.

The crowd dispersed but she clung to him, closer than his very shadow and followed him until he reached a house where he went in. When he sat down she took a place at his feet and, washing them with her tears, dried them with her hair. She kissed and fondled them lovingly. She felt at that hour that she was healed of all her maladies. The light of the new prophet flooded her soul and the mercy of God held her in its embrace. Her pride was purged: regret, sorrow and reproach were gone from her and she had found an utter happiness such as she had never dreamed possible. Her healing brought tears of joy to her eyes. She had no mind for anything but this new faith. She set out into it with all the joy, sincerity and strength she could command. No soul before her had ever been cleansed like hers. Nor had the Divine grace ever filled a soul to overflowing as this young sinful woman's. By God's grace she became a saint: her sanctity was to become proverbial.

# The Christian Soldier

After a few days' absence, the Roman youth was consumed with longing to see the girl from Magdal again. When he returned to the house, he was welcomed by the women in their wonted way, but in answer to his questions they informed him that she had gone out one day without telling anyone what her intentions were. No one knew the reason for her departure nor where she had gone. They said there was nothing surprising about such behaviour on her part. From the first day they had known that she was not their type and that there was some mystery about her. They had not the least doubt that one day she would leave that hell of a place and never return.

The soldier was amazed at what he heard and felt he had lost his dearest treasure. He could not bear to be patient about her. The fact that no one knew anything of her greatly perturbed him and he was distressed by the thought that possibly she had quitted Jerusalem fleeing whence she would not return. He made constant search for her in the city without finding a trace.

While he was roaming the byways of Jerusalem without a clue to follow, he saw a large crowd around the new prophet and following behind him. Having heard much of this prophet and his miracles, he joined the throng to find out what he could. They continued on their way until they came to the house where his followers had established themselves. The occupants came out to greet the teacher, and among them she of Magdal. He was overjoyed, recognising her at once, and he resolved to accost her and tell her that he had come back for her and was still her devoted lover.

He enquired about the house and the household and about the man the people thronged. He heard many things, utterly foreign to him, of which he understood little. But he found out that his beloved had become one of the most ardent and sincere of his followers and that her life was now intimately bound up with the new religion. He formed the belief that she had severed all connection with her former life and from every remembrance of it. Yet as he reflected, it seemed to him that there was no ground for despair in these developments. Was not their mutual love of the purest and noblest kind? There was no reason in what had happened for her to repudiate him. He waited a while for her to come out so that he could talk with her and press his suit on her as he had done before. He had the idea too that he would go inside after her. If she refused him he would leave lest otherwise he should impede her new life. If she received him that would be an indication of her pleasure at his return and their earlier relationship could be resumed.

When she learned of his presence and his efforts and yearning to meet her, she did not turn him away, but invited him in and greeted him. He thought she still regarded him with the same ardent affection. But soon he discovered that her love was no longer just for him. Her welcome was not the sort a girl would give who was delighted at the return of an old lover. Yet she did not rebuff him as one might who feared fresh overtures from a love she no longer acknowledged. What he met with was neither rejection nor affection and it confused and distressed him. In his perplexity he did not know how to interpret her attitude. He had no way of understanding how she could still love him, yet not any longer as a woman loves a man or even as men love each other. Her love for him was simply part of her love for all, a holy love transcending the particular. Though she went on talking to him, his mind wandered. He did not know what to do. He resolved to throw himself at her feet and implore her to return to him, or let him come back to her. But she broke off before he did so, interrupting the train of his thoughts to introduce him to one of the disciples as a promising, well-disposed person. And certainly something in his nature sensed that he was moving toward faith.

He started to make intermittent visits to the disciples as often as he had opportunity. At first they were ill at ease about him, fearing that he was spying on them on behalf of the authorities. He too fraternised with them only to a certain point. He did not listen to much of their conversation and only entered a little into discussion with them. It may well have been that his only objective in seeking them out was the chance to stay near to her he loved.

He found their conversation very tedious, taken up as it was with subjects belonging to faith and belief, the dread of sin and denial of God. He longed for talk like that of his own community about courage, bravery and pleasure. It astounded him to find that they did not believe in force and were utterly devoid of admiration for bravery and appreciation of glory. Everything in which Romans gloried they despised. He could not help wondering whether such a gospel, with its eager brief for forgiveness, could possibly survive. Could those who believed it conceivably withstand the fierce forces that were gathering to their destruction, as long as they did not resist what was inflicted on them, only countering hostility with prayer to God to guide the enemy and forgive him his sin? It was indeed a remarkable religion. Men in power had only to take it seriously and the whole thing would come to an end and become oblivious in oblivion.[11] He had not been thus in their company long before one day he met the master himself. His disciples were with him at the close of a trying day. As soon as the master's glance fell on him he felt as if a light had shined in his heart. His conscience responded to the religion the new prophet had brought and from that time he began rightly to understand it. From that hour he became one of the company of believers.

The conversation had to do with that very day's events. The leaders of Israel were in very angry mood. They had sentenced a woman to be stoned and when the people were about to proceed with the stoning, the Lord Christ had said to them: 'He among you who is without sin let him be the first to stone her.' Softened by these words, the people had slunk away. But it infuriated the leaders, who regarded it as an outrage against the law which would encourage people to flout the commands of the Book, not to mention its implicit disavowal of one of the most fundamental principles of the social order.

As far as the Roman soldier was concerned, the saying fell into good ground. He saw in it the victory of conscience over the established order. In that order he had been reared and he was one of its worshippers. The very life of his people was built upon it. He started to think over it all and began saying to himself: 'If sin is the act of transgressing the bounds set by God then it is for God alone to punish it. It is no business of the sinner's to kill another sinner like himself, even though there be varying degrees of sin. Only those who are free from sin should punish: only they should give judgement. And who of us can claim to be without sin? Anybody making such a claim must be considered to be trespassing on the rights of God, since he arrogates to himself the right to punish sins of which only God knows. He himself, moreover, has committed many sins. To God – all praise and majesty to Him – we must leave the punishment of His servants for their transgressions. With His almighty power and ample knowledge God is well able to do this. He has no need of any of us to implement His will.

'People are liable to confuse contraventions of religion with contraventions of the established order. To punish the former belongs to God alone, only the retribution of the latter is our affair. Only we must administer such penalties in the name of the established order and not in the name of religion. Those who try to sustain the external order with religious sanctions are in error about what religion really is. The external order is the work of humanity. It is imperfect, temporal, subject to change. That cannot possibly be the case with religion. Thus the prohibitions that belong to the social realm must remain a wholly human sphere under safeguards for which we are responsible. It is unjust for us to hide behind religion in order to bolster the external order. That is the practice of many who inflict harsh penalties on wrongdoers in their passionate zeal, not so much for religion, as for the protective preservation of the whole external order, which is our work and may be either right or wrong.'[12]

Somebody in the discussion spoke about the ancient Egyptians, who, he said, were the most ethical of the heathen and very sound in their thinking. However they were ignorant of God and did not realise that He was the source of what was good in themselves. On that account it was their passion to have their names and their deeds endure and be remembered. This supplied a motive force for them to do what was good — witness how they inscribed their names on monuments that time has not obliterated. The naïvete of this idea brought laughter from the audience. It was the best that heathenism could produce. Then the Roman soldier turned the discussion to the Roman leaders and declared that what impelled them to great achievements was their fine and enduring traditions and their sense of history. He considered that this was a splendid thing about the Romans. But the disciples were no less amused. Such notions were not one whit higher than those of other heathen people. Humanity without God is a fit theme for laughter, for then there is no meaning to what we do and no worth in the motive forces from which our deeds derive. It is conscience alone which differentiates us from the beasts. Conscience is God's gift and without God the child of Adam is no more than an intelligent animal. But mankind — it is impossible for him to be, without God.

Reasoning like that appealed to the soldier and he sincerely believed it, to the point that he began to set great value on conscience and to hold the outward system in contempt. He began to understand about God and His ways, His commands and His prohibitions and to distinguish between what was God's (praise and majesty unto Him) and what was ours. What was properly God's alone we had falsely arrogated to ourselves. He began to believe in humility, in absolute good and in forbearance. He realised for the first time the vain and empty things that Romans had stooped to venerate and pursue, and even to die for. He despised glory, greatness and prestige, indeed everything that did not spring from conscience.

He set about preaching these new principles and calling his friends in the forces to adopt them. He sought to convince those closest to him, using, however, the utmost caution. Even so it was not long before the commander came to know that there were ideas going about in the ranks, having to do with the call to mercy, love and forbearance and forbidding to kill. They were disparaging to the imperial order and discredited the glory and greatness of Rome. He resolved to take the situation firmly in hand and to allow no one to filch his army's great name. For it was the very pride of Rome and the object of a universal admiration.

It happened shortly afterward that this captain led an army to a neighbouring city. The soldier who had come to believe in Christ was among those sent out to fight. He did not know what would happen to him. But his spirit was at rest in the conviction that he would never kill anyone, friend or foe, and that he would never permit the rule of authority to tyrannise over his conscience. Yet he had no idea what form this struggle between authority and conscience would take.

# A Sick Girl

Pain at night is pain intensified.

A night of pain is night prolonged.

And such pain – God knows – is in no need of anything to make it more intense.

Nor did that night need any prolonging. The scene was a small dwelling house in one of the quarters of Jerusalem. So secluded were the people of the house and preoccupied tending a sick girl that nobody heard tell of them. And they in their turn knew nothing of the world around them and the events that were happening there. It was plainly a house of the poor, though not chronically or desperately needy. There was no furniture to speak of. But it was not altogether bereft of means to at least a plain and simple life. Theirs was not that utter destitution that generates bitter hatred of one's fellows. On the contrary, they had no rancour in their hearts. The sick girl lay in one of the upper rooms. For some days her pain had been growing worse and had reached a stage more intense than any of them had before experienced.

She was still quite young. As the sickness grew upon her, pallor had given to her skin almost a transparent look. For all its severity, her illness had not robbed her of her goodly appearance, nor, exhausting as it was, did it mar the purity of her face. When the spasms of pain passed her calm composure returned, the composure of a spirit that no distress or weariness could break. Bodily affliction had not changed her character one whit when it had deprived her of the power to move.

Time and again, with alarming intensity, her pain returned and day by day grew sharper. As her family watched her anguish their anxiety became unbearable. They were desperate to find some relief, as she lay racked with agony. Then in the intervals of ease from pain she would amaze them with her power of recovery, her composure and clear thoughts.

But when the pain returned in all its force it was unbearable for those around her to see her so tormented. One of the women (none other than Mary herself) besought one of the disciples to go to the Lord Christ and ask him to heal the girl. He was a disciple who never refused any directive or wish of Mary's. She told him: 'Tell Christ she is the daughter of my neighbour and friend. She's a very good-hearted person, one of the best. It can't be that God wills such pain for one like her. Tell him she's suffered as none ever did before that we heard of. When God bestowed on him the power to heal the sick, He did so for the sake of just such a pure and gentle soul as she who lies so ill.'

A friend of the family who heard of her illness directed them to a traveller who had visited many parts of India and had brought back from there a herb called opium. When taken it has a magic effect in alleviating pain. When they tried the sample he brought them, the results were amazing. In a few minutes the pain was gone as if she had not been ill a day.

No one was more delighted or relieved because of this medicine than the girl's mother. She was a very gentle woman, of delicate physique and fine-featured, with a quiet voice that in her sharpest moments was never raised to a higher pitch than most people's in ordinary conversation. God had blessed both her and her daughter with the inestimable gift of diffusing around them a quiet serenity that pervaded everyone who came into contact with them, without exception. A very active, noisy child in the house, who was very disobedient and fractious, used to quieten down at a glance from the sick girl and he would climb on to her bed and sit beside her as meekly as could be, and behave very gently with her. When some of the folk had the idea of locking the door of the sick room to keep him out, he made angry protests and threatened anyone who might do so again. He seemed to be afraid that someone would do her harm unless he kept watch over her.

Everyone in the house felt there was a wonderful kinship of spirit between the child and the sick girl. It was as if age had nothing to do with spiritual relationships and that disparity in years was of no significance in unity of soul.

Night fell while the patient slept from the effect of the drug. Those who use opium for the relief of pain sleep in a strange manner. From their faces they seem to be almost in a wakeful state, as if it were only the body that slumber touches, while the soul remains as wide awake as ever. The spirit may not respond but it seems to be listening, or so at least it appears to the watcher by the bed.

The household went about its preparations in readiness for when she awoke. They had to bring her food in the intervals between sleep. When she awoke she was quite free from pain and she had none of that sleepy drowsiness on waking of people who are reluctant to be aroused. She opened her eyes wide and was at once fully alert, as if slumber as a veil had been lifted from her. She smiled as if she had never known any pain. Those around her set about helping her to move her position and take what little food she could. As they seated her comfortably, they rejoiced she had come back to them and yet hardly believed it. It was on her mind that she should thank the friend who had brought her the medicine. But she only smiled. Then she remarked that it was bad of her not to forget wrongs and to forgive those who had done them to her. Nobody understood to whom she referred in saying this for nobody with her knew of any wrong he had done her any time, whether great or small. Strong misgivings came over them for it was the sort of remark a person might well make on the brink of death. As they gazed at her she smiled with such a look of sincerity and exoneration that they were reassured and took it that she only meant to refer to her own thoughts about herself that had been wrong and to make it plain she did not deludedly think, as some do, that she was perfect. She talked in pleasant, almost playful, tones to those around her. But as the pain steadily returned and her voice weakened, she lapsed into silence. The watchers knew that in a very few moments she would be in agony again. It beset her body first and there was a little, varying, hiatus before the spirit also was drawn into the vortex and one anguish tortured soul and body. I know of nothing that produces that interlude in the way intense suffering does. The body suffers excruciating pain while the spirit, by its own force, wins a brief respite from the onset. It is a strange hiatus between body and spirit. Perhaps it is this phenomenon which gives rise to the widely held belief that great suffering refines and purifies the soul, since the strength of the soul is then triumphantly surmounting the body's pain and holding off from its weariness. But the fact is that this is only true during that brief interval. When it is over, pain is sheer torment, nothing more.[13]

The girl's cries increasing, the mother asked about the drug and was told that it was finished. She was beside herself as she replied: 'If somebody doesn't bring her this medicine I'll batter her head in with my own hands. I'd rather do that than see her suffer as she did before.' Her words fell ominously on the whole company. The pained silence hanging over the house seemed to deepen as she spoke and her trembling cry, as it faded, seemed to hang in the silence too, like a mocking echo.

They reassured her they were certain they would soon have some more medicine. Not one of them but was distraught as they heard fresh outbursts of crying. The fearful vigil in which they were caught cast a growing terror into their hearts.

That very moment there came a knock at the door. It was almost as if an angel from heaven had descended upon them. They snatched the medicine and made her swallow the dose. After a few minutes the patient grew quiet, her cries becoming more intermittent and diminishing in intensity. As the pain passed altogether the tempest gave way to complete calm and under the opium she slept deeply. The lights were extinguished and silence descended on the house. All went off to find some sleep before the paroxysms of pain began anew.

One night they had an instinctive feeling that she would not live to see the dawn. What were they to bear such a burden but a group of frail and feeble women folk and one small child?

It was that night they received a visit from the disciple whom the Lord Christ loved and whom the lady Mary had sent to him in hope of the patient's being healed at his hands. The disciple came with the Lord's answer to this yearning desire.

'My master says that your sick daughter is clean from all sin, pure from all transgression. He says too that though he is commissioned to guide the sick in soul and bring them forgiveness of their sins, he has only been directed to bestow bodily healing and raise the dead when such miracles are among the signs of God by which He wills to bring men and women into faith. He has no mandate to interrupt the Divine law in the physical realm when some breakdown in it leads to disease.'

'Do you think, then, that God wills this girl, in her innocence and purity, to suffer agony the like of which no one before has witnessed, when great sinners elsewhere jest and sport in full enjoyment of their health and happiness? One of the reasons that induce people to seek to be pure is that purity is a factor in their good health and well being. Pain has no justification except as retribution for the sin of the evil doer. It is criminals who deserve it. If pain, as you say, cleanses and purifies the soul from the defilements of prosperity and the temptations of good health so that it becomes the road to paradise, then pain should be the lot of those who are in need of cleansing. It is not right that it should single out the innocent. Are we not induced to keep clear of evil by the fact that the evil doer incurs punishment and thereby loss of health and happiness? Or conversely, are we not encouraged to well doing by the fact that those who do well are secure from retribution and pain in this world?'

'God does not reward purity of soul with bodily well being, nor does He requite the sin of the spirit with disease of the body. These fantasies belong to those who measure His knowledge by their ignorance. Rewards are surely in the same realm as the deeds they concern. Punishment is only just when it is a natural consequence of transgression. Injustice is not an attribute of God. If God were to punish unbelievers with bodily afflictions, that would be unjust. Rather He requites them with restlessness of conscience. Pain in point of fact is neither retribution nor catharsis. It is the natural result of malfunctioning in the body which has nothing to do with the soul. The ill which befalls believers is neither a trial of faith, nor yet a paving of the way to paradise. There is no causal relation between faith and health. If things were as you think them to be, the requital of every evil deed would be speedy sickness and the reward of good, uninterrupted good health. Then everybody would be commendable believers. God has not willed such a pattern of things in the law of His creation.'

'The wisdom that is God's we cannot fathom. Nor can we illuminate its far reaches. But I am fearful lest people develop wrong notions about your master. I am afraid they may doubt his Divinity and even his being a prophet. Soon they may be doubting even his humanity.'

'My lady, you have been talking very sharply about him and because of that sharp remark in a moment of weariness he said: "Woman what is there between me and thee?" It is a saying that will be puzzling people centuries hence.'[14]

At this the sleeping patient awoke and interjected – as if she had been listening to everything that was being said around her: 'I know what the master Christ said about me. I know without a doubt that I am safe, that I am guiltless and pure. For it was he who described me so. I could not have coveted in life any greater happiness than to have him speak thus of me. It is all the same to me now whether I die or recover. I am satisfied in that he called me a believer. I seek no reward for this faith. Nor do I want my sickness to be treated as a kind of test case of his truthfulness. In any event, he is faithful and true: that is my conviction. You must not judge what he does by what others do. All he does is well, even though it seems outwardly far other than you would wish.'

She tried to sit but could not. She fell with her head on the pillow in a little tremor. Her body drooped and her head bowed in death. They all rushed to her but she was beyond their aid.

It was the woman from Magdal who came and shrouded her and gave her the parting kiss. She had been the gentlest of nurses and had kept a steady vigil over her. Now, when tenderness could do no more, she left her and, going to the apostle, enquired of him in great distress what the people had done with her lord. She was back again in that customary preoccupation of mind in which she could think of no one else.

The apostle would say nothing, restrained by sorrow from opening up any conversation. It seemed to her that he went in dread of something impending. She took hold of his two side locks of hair and shook his head roughly, demanding of him what lay behind this silence. Did he think anything had befallen the master? Could it be that his enemies had laid evil hands upon him? He did not speak. But her mood of passionate indignation would brook no denial. He was compelled to relate to them what the people of Israel had done and their decision to get the Romans that day to have him crucified on a charge of blasphemy.

'Christ is to be crucified for denying God? Shall it then ever be said again that we are rational beings with a conscience? Shall we be expected ever to rely again on human wisdom?'

The amazing thing is that nothing about it all dismays him. He is steadfast as a mountain, imperturbable, serene. He has no will to indicate what we may do to rescue him. Yet he knows we are pledged to do his bidding though it means that we all perish.'

'Does that mean that you will have nothing to say against this monstrous deed, that you'll take no action on his behalf?'

'He himself declares that it is the will of God and that we have no right to impede His decree and purpose.'

'But surely when God gave us reason, He entered under covenant to give us understanding of His wisdom. If we are denied the light of it, we may find ourselves in such a pitch of doubt as to be hardly better than downright unbelief.'

'Hold on to your faith. For only in adversities is it known for what it is. And we, heaven knows, are in unparalleled adversity. Let us hold fast to our belief. It may be that God will guide us on the true path, and not bring unbelief and error upon us.'

Most of the women there did not at first realise the gravity of the news which the disciple brought. It had taken them so

## With the Disciples

completely by surprise that they were stunned. Then it began to dawn on them how tragically it would affect them to lose their dearest friend on earth, simple, frail women as they were, and worn down by sleepless sorrow and suffering. They broke down into bitter tears, wailing loudly, until Mary rebuked them sharply. Her remonstrance brought them round to a more proper composure. She herself had taken the desperate news quietly and calmly. A slight tightening of her lips was the only evident sign of her grief. She was still the same great-souled person, dignified and clearsighted, despite everything. God had bestowed on her a peace for heaven, a special benison upon one whom He had chosen before all the women of the world.

The girl from Magdal had no such capacity for patience. She could not imagine life without him who had delivered her from a tormented conscience and from the sin of pride. She could no longer live save by him and for him. She resolved even at the cost of her life to shield him from the Roman forces. What was life worth without him? But in the weight of her sorrow she fainted and they laid her on her bed. The women did not dare to hope she would come through such grief alive.

The disciple went on in deepening anguish of spirit and came to a nearby house where the disciples were assembled debating what it was their duty to do on that day of crisis.

# The Disciples in Conference

The disciples came together that night to consider what action ought to be taken now that the people of Israel and the Romans had agreed to crucify Christ. There was no more high-souled or great-hearted group of men on the face of the earth than they, and none more well intentioned. They talked together of how they could uphold what was indubitably right and how they could obviate gross and undoubted wrong. They were in no sense feeble in their conviction, or irresolute. Nor were they intimidated by danger. They were not given to unruly passion nor to the self-will that might have diverted them from the path of right. On the contrary, they were motivated by strong, pure, disinterested love. In the long debates in which they engaged, argument was sharp among them as they exchanged mutual recriminations, of which, God knows, they were innocent. Indeed, only their strength of faith and sincerity of purpose had preserved them from intrusive hatreds. Sharp differences of view arose despite their piety and devotion, their self-sacrifice and high dedication.

Perhaps in that circumstance there is ground to make us pause critically over the view that to bring together a group of people with the same outlook necessarily creates among them a common front or mutual cohesion and shared reactions such as to ensure common attitudes. And it is all the same whether those assemblies consist of disciples, or idolaters, learned doctors or ignorant folk, criminals or men of piety. It is not long before they give evidence of being the same mixture, some enterprising and lethargic, adventurous and cautious, advocates of boldness and advocates of prudence, some given to haste, others to long range plans, near-sighted and far-sighted. You have all these disparities whatever be the theme of debate. Agreement is not readily reached on the part of people like these, unless it be of a precarious sort.

There were ten disciples in the meeting. The traitor had departed and the beloved disciple was absent because they had sent him to the master to bring back word of him and to ascertain his wishes. They had with them one of the Magi whom they knew well and greatly esteemed. He was one of the three who had come to Bethlehem at the birth of Christ, following a star to which their knowledge guided them as it shone in the heavens, until it directed them to his birthplace. Then they observed that the star increased in brilliance, reaching its brightest on the day of the sermon on the mount. Two of the Magi were present then. As thereafter the star grew dim they knew that Christ's sojourn on the earth was nearing its end. The youngest of the three remained to witness the final eclipse of the light which for so long had guided him.

The disciples spent more than a little time going to and from their minds over all that had happened. They were in the deepest distress, each in his own mind brooding over their sorrow and desperation or turning it over in debate with one another. Yet no line of thought emerged clearly before them and no line of action found formulation.

Then the doyen of them, the bearer of the keys, spoke up and said:

'We are today confronting the sorest trial we have ever undergone. The turmoil of grief and sorrow that has seized you will avail nothing in this catastrophe. Those things will get us nowhere. I fear for you unless remorse and regret give way to resolve and action. We can be troubled in soul to such a point that we have no strength left when our conscience summons us to serious action. When that happens our staying power will fail us and our mind will be incapable of seeing the true shape of our duty, of facing things decisively and resolving on a clear course of action. Then we will find peace for our spirit, however fraught with danger our decision may be and however exacting our undertaking. So I bid you rid yourselves of your present frame of mind and think calmly about what action we ought to take tomorrow. Irresolution and perplexity take a greater toll of mental and inward balance than does the worst exposure to physical dangers.'

There was silence for a while as they got into a quieter frame of mind, then one of them said:

'The sin that is to be done tomorrow is the foulest ever to be committed by humanity in all its sin-laden history. People have never been so far from the right as they are in this. They have confused the best of men with the worst and made prophets equal with brigands. This is a dastardly deed. But it cannot be laid at the door of one group only or of one particular community. The guilt of it falls upon everybody. If we deliver the Lord Christ we shall be delivering humanity as a whole from a burden under which it would groan to all eternity.'

Another disciple said:

'It would indeed be good for us to deliver him, and all humanity with him, from an unparalleled crime. But even more is it incumbent upon us to rescue him, out of sheer love for him. He who does not offer his life in the cause of the one he loves has no love at all for him. And any one who has no love is not one of us. Nor is he of our company whose faith does not override a mere desire for security. I am going to intervene between him and his unjust oppressors. They are not to be compared with the thongs of his shoes. I will challenge the forces that are set to do him evil. Either I save him from them, or they destroy me. If I die I will be content to do so. If I save him, what bliss, now and hereafter.'

Another said:

'But do you not think that it would be equally fitting we should save and defend even an ordinary person from so foul a deed being perpetrated on him? It is the evident enormity of the thing itself about which our conscience refuses to be silent. If we are not passionate about justice anywhere, what is the point of talking about right and wrong and justice? Unless we repel the detestable thing with hand and tongue, it doesn't help anyone that we repudiate it in our hearts. Love of justice, and that alone, lays on us the solemn duty of making our indignation effective on behalf of him who is oppressed, whatever his status and however virulently he is hated. If this is so, how much more then when the victim of foul wrong is the best of all humanity, the dearest and most beloved to our hearts? If you want your faith in truth and justice to have any meaning you must defend him against the evil of the men of iniquity. In default of such action you pronounce judgement on your own selves that your creed is a delusion and your faith a wisp.'

Yet another said:

'I am with you, in your passionate zeal for him, for humanity and for justice. But you have forgotten that the primary consideration making his deliverance our duty is our obligation to be vigilant and jealous for the religion he inaugurated. There is not one of us who can preach it after him as he does. Men will not follow any of us as they follow him. There cannot be the least doubt that if these blood-shedding rulers destroy him they will wipe out this precious religion. Our shame when they see our failure to defend our prophet will further increase our incapacity to proclaim his message. His life in itself alone is more competent to bring about the fulfilment of the peace for which the world yearns and for its guidance than the lives of all of us without him.'

And another disciple said:

'This is undoubtedly right and well said. But I would go further and add that if you are concerned to safeguard the religion, the plan should certainly be to do so by delivering the master forcibly. Persuasion and petitioning for mercy, talk about justice and love, are not the way. Already we have been a heavy drawback to him in his mission. Have not people said that if he were any good he would have had other followers than the riff-raff of our society. We are already quite despicable enough in their eyes. Did they not dub us the dregs of the population and say that God does not guide the people of Israel by means of a gang of fishermen from Galilee?

'As long as we were with him people could say what they liked about us. His presence among us was enough to make us a match for the whole world. But if he is no longer in our midst we will never succeed after him, unless people are assured that we were acting submissively, before, only out of deference to his authority; and that, acknowledging no other lordship, we then held off from resisting them, not out of fear or cowardice but out of identification with him and out of rejection for his sake of the world's ways, and in loyalty to the religion in which he believed.'

Another said:

'Strength and weakness in the world's eyes really depend upon whether or not a person is clearly willing to face death. Don't you agree that the reason why some rider to battle is so awe-inspiring that thousands of free men worship him is just that he alone is ready to die and by that circumstance contrives to lead them and escapes death into the bargain?

'Let no one on any account say that we are too weak to warrant any hope of success. If we shrink from defending him our enemies will take revenge on us and they'll leave us only the alternative of death or undying shame and disgrace. If they treat us leniently our life after that will be contemptible. Such capitulation on our part to falsehood will be unbelief. If we act boldly people will remember our action with pride and admiration, and if we die posterity will have us in honoured memory. Who has greater glory than the man who, despite his being aware of his weakness, is ready to be killed in the cause of truth and justice?'

Their corporate enthusiasm grew to a high pitch and the weight of despair was lifted from their spirits. Their hearts beat high with courage and they rejoiced in their new found resolve after the bitter taste of vacillation and perplexity. They were of one mind to take every possible means to save him.

After a silent pause one of them declared:

'My proposal is that we snatch him tonight from prison. The guards are not numerous and it will not be difficult to overpower them even if one or two who challenge us are killed. Or it may be a better idea to wait until the soldiery goes up the mountain and attack them then. We shall get away with him quite easily.'

Naturally there was an intoxicating feeling in the desire for bold action after they had spent so much time in inactivity, preoccupied with matters of dogma and belief. It was natural too that they should have sensed the need to demonstrate their strength and tenacity. For these hitherto had not been conspicuous. It was natural too that they should have in common a longing to be rid of their past – a thing which is not always easy. To resolve on active and decisive steps was a source of real satisfaction to them. None of them doubted that, resorting as they would to force, they might well be obliged in doing so to face death and what to them was worse than death, namely the killing of innocent men among their adversaries.

Their arguments came thick and fast and with increasing force. They followed each other in a sort of mounting crescendo, just as waves, though they be weak ones, gather increasing strength if they move rhythmically and steadily, whereas even high waves diminish and weaken when they beat hither and thither. In a community like theirs the points of debate interacted sharply, the weak arguments gathering strength by their sheer accumulation, and strong arguments losing force when they did not sustain each other.

So their determination to give battle and to resist by force increased, to the point where it became difficult for any one of them to counter and oppose it in its full tide. They were almost in a fever of excitement. Some of them imagined themselves arming with swords and rubbed their hands as if warming up for the fight.

At this point one of them spoke up, in some fear.

'You know well enough that I am not a craven-hearted fellow or lustful to live. Nor do I doubt that what we have said tonight is true and right. But while our master is alive among us I do not want to contravene a command of his. My faith in him is all I have in this world. I would not wish to die having gone counter to him in anything, great or small. I cannot be guided in any matter whatsoever except by him. You know well that when the armed guards came out to take him and the people clamoured against him he commanded us not to resist them or harm them. You remember too how he remonstrated with one of us who drew his sword and struck the ear of one of the soldiers. His command to us then was crystal clear. However right any action seems to me I will never go ahead with it unless you bring me authorisation from him. If he is no longer with us tomorrow, tomorrow I will then allow myself to determine things by my reason, on condition that I do not go against conscience. But today he remains both my reason and my conscience. If you are wanting me to set our ideas above his commandments, I would in that case be giving my reason precedence over my religion and that is something I cannot countenance.'

Another disciple rebutted him saying: 'Do you want him to have to say to us: Die to defend me? That is what emperors and other stony-hearted men will say. It is not likely that he, with his tender heart of compassion, will order us to die on his behalf, even when we are well assured that we are in the right and they in the wrong. It isn't our job to consent cheerfully to shame and perfidy. We are not bound to obey him on the question of whether he should be rescued. To deliver him is an absolute good that nothing can disqualify.'

'I would be opposed to rescuing him if that should involve us in the use of force. For that is the very thing he has forbidden us. My view is that our religion has not given to conscience unlimited authority but authorises us to act as reason indicates while remaining within the limits that conscience does cover, however desirable it may seem to be to transgress them. Religion has to do with limits and prohibitions rather than with right guidance and positive commands.'

'This notion of yours is weak to the point of near treachery. It is open to such vacillation that it is almost stupid. Would not a successful outcome for us be also the victory of religion? What then is the point of your impeding a religious victory in the name of religion?'[15]

'I have no desire to perpetrate a crime for the sake of making religion secure. Religion has a Lord Who is well able to secure it, and has no need to require a transgression on my part in the worthy cause. Such fantasies are the product of the feeble in faith who are half-baked in their religiosity.'

'God makes us factors in the execution of His will. It is up to us to guard jealously the security of religion.'

'Are we more concerned for religion than he is? Do you know better what befits the spread of his gospel than he does? You look upon his being taken from us as destructive of religion. That is what we think. It may or may not be so. But to use violence is a plain rebellion against his word. This is a matter of conscience and Divinely decreed. To defy it is in my view the worst presumption.'

'Of course it is permissible to depart from religious principles for the sake of defending religion itself. There is, for example, no alternative but to destroy false belief by death, if such false belief is seditious. Sedition is a worse evil than killing.'

'Well, alleged heresy may or may not be heresy: but murder is a definite transgression of religion which no exegesis can sustain. It is not a matter of differing opinions. Doubtless action aimed at the destruction of the faith is a worse evil than death. But it must in truth be action destructive of the faith, and that is precisely what it is so difficult to be sure about. Killing, however, is an evil about which there's no uncertainty once it has been done. You consider that leaving him to his fate would be a flagrant dereliction of duty. But is it not possible that our abstaining from his rescue today is one of the fundamental principles of religion, having to do with atonement for sins? Conspiracy against the faith is truly worse than killing, if the conspiracy is established. But establishing it requires proof and it is just there that one can be right or wrong. But there are no two ways about killing and violence. They are incontrovertibly evil and neither probable good nor anticipated evil justify them as a policy to follow.'

'Religion in no way enjoins us to ignore our reason to that extent.'

'Religion commands you to obey your reason unless your conscience tells you to desist. When your conscience says: "Stop" there is no option but to obey. Our master, who is our conscience, has forbidden us to use force, even in the interests of his victory or the victory of the faith.'

'But Moses killed people and did so in order to bring them into religion and truth.'

'Moses fought to safeguard his nation from the hostility of their enemies. It may be that this hostility derived from religious otherness. But it was at all events hostility. Self-defence is permissible if there is verified hostility, on condition that you are not yourself the originator of the enmity in precaution against some anticipated ill-will. Moses, however, did not make war to propagate religion nor to resist deviations from the faith. He only slew the worshippers of the calf because they violated the law and flouted his authority, he being a ruler; and rulers have the right to require obedience. Once in control again, he did not let his enmity against them enter into the religious realm. The rest of the prophets who took up the sword resembled him in this. They only took it up in self-protection and to safeguard their people from their enemies. None of the prophets compelled any community into embracing faith by dint of the sword, for there can be no forcible recruitment into religion.'

'We today have nothing to do with this exegetical discussion. The point is that if we refrain from delivering him, it will be a catastrophe for him, for us and for religion.'

'Is there no way open to us of saving him without resort to force?'

'Do you remember the Roman soldier who attended our sessions? It was clear that he knew the difference between good and evil and that he believed in peace. Can we not seek out his help to prevent his brother soldiers of Rome from perpetrating this foul deed, or at least to persuade them to leave him in our hands to flee, he and we, from this city of wrong?'

'That would be a treachery to his nation which I would not wish us to ask of him. I am terribly afraid that we are slipping into the depths of sin. When we reach the lowest point we will find no easy way back to salvation.'

'I heard that some time ago he was accused of betraying his army and his nation on the field of battle, and that he will be condemned today. Most people think he will be put to death in the most fearful manner as a penalty for his treachery.'

Their enthusiasm ebbed away and they were back again in their old state of hesitation and distress. Gone was the exultation they had felt when they agreed to take definite action to resist the monstrous wrong. They were angry with those who had kindled these new doubts after they had brought themselves to the point of being assured that it was right to take up the fight. If the arguments calling for brave action were in need of going over again in order that they might be sharpened and corroborated, did not those advocating inaction decline all too readily into the abyss of total negation?

The summons to positive action is always easier for the advocate than the summons to reflection, even if, at the hour of actual translation into fulfilment, the former is more difficult. The call to abstain from action is harder to advocate but easier to obey. A positive line of action makes the spirit more assured, and brings a psychological satisfaction which controversy only intensifies. For this reason such a policy is easier and more satisfying both for him who sponsors it and for those he calls upon to follow it. The negative or inactive approach, however, puts its advocate into a position where he is suspect.

Thus it requires courage and sincerity and yet offers no occasion for exuberance, since its implementation calls for no display of bravery whatsoever.

Men take a different attitude to duty when they are discussing it from when they are face to face with acting on their decision. The spokesman for a brave front may well be the least courageous of men when the time for action arrives, though the fact would argue no necessary cowardice or hypocrisy on his part. Similarly the protagonist of inaction may well be the bravest of men without his bravery amounting to any assured conviction about the rightness of what he does. It is simply a phenomenon that is in the nature of public gatherings where men come together for full discussion. It is most likely that the point of view demanding bold action, even if it be mistaken, will prevail over the view that calls for restraint, however right it be. And it will fall out so, irrespective of whether the partisans of bold action are actually by temperament resolute in action or not. Such is the nature of corporate consultation when it is worked out in this form in a great society. It would seem that there is no guarantee of valid ideas or of immunity from mistakes, even though the men who compose these bodies are the manner of men the disciples were, thoroughly well intentioned, sincerely religious and most zealous in faith. Yet despite all these qualities, when they consulted together they were in no way different from any other community council. Such bodies are not a means of neutralising wrong thinking.

Anger over the waverers prompted one of the disciples to resume the debate. He said:

'Who in any case is going to benefit from renunciation of force? Those most likely to use violence are the wicked doers, and their violence and evil alike are only increased against the good when the latter affirm non-violence. In this manner they leave an open field for these criminals to despoil them with impunity, without fear of retaliation or of force to counter force. It is precisely the best of people who have no need of the gospel of non-violence. Force is something they will never misuse, while non-violence is something the evil doers will never respond to. I can see nothing but danger in this absolute veto on the appeal to force.'

'Well, I at least shall get from it the satisfaction of having obeyed God and having shunned what He has forbidden us. And more than this, as I see it, no man can desire.'

'As if the only thing to be desired was to secrete oneself in a monastery or live in a mountain and leave others to do the sinning and the erring.'

'Of course not. I want people to live together in communities, actively striving to bring their life and work as individuals within the limits of obedience toward God. And if they want to be sacrificial let them sacrifice themselves not others.'

'Were we not ashamed when the people saw us fleeing when he was arrested?'

Whereupon their leader spoke:

'I am indeed as much ashamed of that now as I would be of downright unbelief. I have never been so humiliated either in my own eyes or before others as I was then. I wanted to use my sword – though I am no swordsman. But I only made people laugh and failed miserably. Anybody attempting an unwonted task, even though it be a right one, is exposed to two dangers, the danger of false appearances and the danger of failure. Those among us who are not practised in taking the sword and in force and who are not temperamentally suited to doing battle with men had better steer well clear of what they are not good at. Being true, in the widest meanings of the term, namely the proper correspondence between one's life and the natural characteristics that make up one's constitution, is the primary secret of a fine and happy life.

'I was almost stunned the day the master told me that I would deny him three times before the morning cock crew. I knew within myself that I would never deny him. But when it happened I discovered my inward frailty despite all my brave resolves. Talk and thought both lie but action does not. He who seeks to give an impression of courage when he is a coward ends up with two disappointments, one in himself and the other in what he does. Most of us are conscientious men of faith: we had better stick to our last, be what we were made to be, and not cross swords with those who are habitués of war with its alarums and excursions. I do not mind admitting to you that I, at all events, was not made for this sort of conflict, though I trust that God will grant me power to enable me to struggle in another way in His cause.

'Truly I find there is much weakness in me. Did not the master teach us to love our enemies? Perhaps in love of my enemies I have succeeded, but I find it difficult to love his enemies, those who treat him so wrongfully. But that I consider is a weakness. I think we are bound to obey him if his command to us is clear and altogether unambiguous. If he has forbidden us to use force to bring his cause to success it is incumbent on us not to transgress his prohibitions.'

'I see between us no difference of view, except in regard to the means and the extent to which we concede to ourselves the right to use force. My opinion is that we should not let ourselves be mastered by anger and hatred. If we do so we will transgress our religion. Let us so order this issue that we do not involve ourselves in the sin of violence.'

'All that is fine so long as it is not inspired by cowardice and weakness. If any of you senses that he holds this view out of fear or apprehension then it is the counsel of Satan. But if it issues from faith and conviction it is the counsel of God. For we may do the same things from two entirely contrasted impulses, the one the inspired revelation of God and the other the wily suggestiveness of Satan. Though there is of course a vast difference between our actions, we may be aware of no difference at all.'

'Are you of the opinion that we should take the line dictated by fear, knowing it to be Satanic, if it coincides with what the prophet enjoined? Or should we abandon it as long as the incentive to it is an evil thing? Do I disobey the prophet in his good commandment, if I feel in the depth of my soul that I am only impelled to do so by hatred and spite?'

'It is your business to obey the prophet and to cleanse your soul from Satanic motives.'

'What is the point of cleansing the motives so long as the action is one and the same?'

'The point is that motives have an abiding effect in the soul beyond the actual doing of the deed. From one and the same action you will find contrasted consequences in the soul, tending toward evil if the motives were evil and to good if they were good, all depending on the incentives in the heart.'

The wise man who was their guest sat silently listening to their discussion without making his views known. But at this point he intervened to say, while they gave him close attention:

'Much of what I have heard has surprised me. I have been apprehensive to see how far short you come in fulfilling the sermon on the mount. We listened to it and understood its import and I thought that it had penetrated your innermost souls and purified your conscience. I was convinced none of you would take a course of action inconsistent with its principles. Now I realise that you still regard it only as a noble exhortation whose directives are to be followed only when feasible, and neglected when they conflict with the weakness and evil in human nature.

'I have also noted in much of what you have said that the emotions actuating you are not such as the master commended to you. In other people who have not listened to the master or known his guiding word, they might well be the most lofty sentiments. But in your case, your motives must be absolutely irreproachable. Motives are worthy or detestable, according to whether they coincide with or contravene conscience. I have heard you argue that it is your love for the master Christ that compels you to take reprisals against those who wrong him. But the real truth is that what drives you to them is hatred of his foes, not love for him. These two are sharply contrasted, though it is often supposed that they are mutually necessary. In their confusion of this score, people imagine that love on their part for a friend can only be by dint of their hating his enemy. To love one's country, for example, means, on this view, hating its enemies. But in fact there is a vast difference between the two attitudes. Love never invites to evil. If I find love calling for evildoing I know that in the heart of the person in question it has turned into hatred of his enemy. This is an error into which most people fall. You must be wary of it. So easy is the confusion that only a very fine sensitivity of conscience is aware of it, and is zealously vigilant for the good in all its purity.

'You have invoked also the principle of the triumph of the right through force. But what else is this on your part but a confusing of right with power? It is a delusion into which most people fall. Right recognises itself as bound by obligations; indeed it could be said in its very nature to be these limits. Force, however, in the nature of the case overreaches these limits as far as it can go. Those who defend the right by force, only do so until they gain their end. Then force alone becomes their master passion. Claims about force as the means to right are usually shortlived claims. They last only a while. Then force, in full career, needs no sanction from right. All who have recourse to force as a means to the right soon discover that they have merely invoked the right as a means to force. So the idea that what is manifestly right should be defended by force should have no place in your motivation. Otherwise your fate will be that when you have righted the right you will be resting upon force alone. That is precisely what your religion forbids.

'You should realise that as long as the right is put in an inferior position it is all the same whether it be force or falsehood to which it is made subservient.

'Furthermore, I heard some of you remark that fear of what people say of you was a motive for action to be taken. It is true enough that there are those who believe that fear of this kind is a powerful factor in inducing people to do what is right. The error is very prevalent. Fear of being thought ill of is a very different thing from the desire after virtue. Such fear, as is the case with hatred, may sometimes lead to admirable actions and then quite soon after lead irretrievably to evil. It is in no way fitting that what you do should be motivated by fear.

'Then too I heard one of you taking pride in his bravery and readiness for sacrifice, out of his anxiety for a good reputation and prestige. One of you remarked that you would find a place in history and that posterity would hold you for ever in glorious remembrance. This is indeed a strange motive for action, though by many it is highly valued as an incentive to well-doing. But it is a pagan way of talking: it is the very sort of hollow vaunting and self-magnification the master forbade you. It is a stupid impulse by which only fools are guided. It has no validity as a motive for goodness, but is, in fact, very close to evil.

'I have no wish to summon you to any particular line of action or to urge any course upon you. You know better than I the issues before you and are more competent to decide them. But I warn you: watch yourselves, scrutinise the motives behind what you do. If they are evil you will ultimately land in evil, even though you have been motivated by immediate good. I warn you against force and where it may lead you. If you kill or harm anyone in going through with what force prescribes, you will thereby transgress the bounds of conscience. That is the supreme disloyalty to your religion, whatever justification you may think you have for it.

'On the point raised by some of you as to the role of that reason with which God has endowed us and the place of our freewill, if it is our job to ignore our reason in plain issues like this one, my view is that you should be guided by reason so long as it keeps within the limits of conscience. You must understand that there are laws which the soul must not transgress unless it is to suffer disease. For in that respect the soul resembles the body though, of course, the principles of soul health are more subtle and less easily understood. The harm too that results from flouting them is less evident than the diseases of the body and more far-reaching. The true unison of our powers of choice, the obligations under which we are laid by these laws of the soul and the behests of reason, is the problem of problems in human life. It may bring the problem home to our minds if we borrow the parable of a man in a boat. He has full freedom of movement and action, as his mind and his reason may determine, but always on condition that he stays within the boat and the limits of the laws of nature that relate to it. Otherwise he will drown.'

At this point the disciple returned whom they had sent to the master to find out his mind and bring back to them his directions. They clamoured around him for news each hoping that his opinion would be the one to be vindicated. The messenger said: 'He commands you to go aside for worship and prayer and to leave him until God fulfills His purpose for him. He bids you go abroad into the world calling men to his truth. He says he will meet you after three days in one of the villages of Galilee and that whatever be the suffering that befalls him on the morrow it is by the will of God and it is not for us to resist it. He warns you against violence and reproaches you for your attitudes at the time of his arrest.'

When they knew that these were his definite instructions and that they were final, their minds were put to rest in that they had a directive they could not possibly transgress. But the decision threw them into profound sorrow, whether their policy had been action or inaction, violence or non-resistance. Equally hard on all was this call for surrender and acquiescence in the worst. Many of them wept.

They had no compensating satisfactions, such as come with decisive action – the thrill of sacrifice in the cause of truth and the lust of revenge on the enemies of religion. Faith and obedience – these only were left to them. They submitted to his command with sorrowing and despairing hearts. They made up their minds to leave Jerusalem, the city of wrong. But there was in their hearts an utter sadness, a regretful reproach, at being obliged to abandon their prophet to the clutches of evil men, who would wreak their will on him. They were wellnigh broken at the thought of this inescapable choice between tragic inaction and the violation of their prophet's will.

The messenger said to them:

'I paid the closest attention to what he said. My view is that we should occupy ourselves wholly in worship and prayer, however distraught by anxiety we may be. We must be led by that mountain sermon. It proved so grievous to us that we forgot it, or so exacting that we pretended to. Maybe it is well for us to heed the words of this wise man. He drank in that sermon and believed what it said with a far firmer faith than ours. It is our duty to follow his advice and wisdom.'

When they heard that, they clung all the more wistfully to this man of wisdom, so untroubled by doubt and distress or indecision. They clung as a drowning man might to his rescuer. They sensed that somehow his absolute faith would be their refuge, that they would find in him the inspiration to lighten, perhaps, the burden of grief during three long days. Through these they had to await their master's return, God having meanwhile raised him to Himself. They gave themselves to prayer and devotion seeking respite thus from the bitter weight of grief they bore.

There can be no doubt that the decision of the disciples was the right one, by the criteria of revelation and religion, and by reference to the things that transcend the capacity of the human mind fully to understand. Nor is there any doubt that they were mistaken in fearing the collapse of the Christian religion when

# With the Disciples

their master was no more with them. In fact by this action of theirs in holding back from forcibly inducing his victory, they rendered a great service to the Christian message. In that day's events, the Christian religion defined its principles and formulated its philosophy. Its dominant characteristics were there and then fashioned. It was those events which gave rise to the most impressive of its tenets about forgiveness and redemption. From them came also that sadness which is a ruling element in the character of the greatest adherents of Christianity, their fear of sin, their love of self-reproach and abasement, their sense of the importance of the sin of Adam and their belief that it had to do with the anguish Christ underwent that humankind might be saved from its consequences. Perhaps all these hallmarks of Christianity are simply an echo of the great sin of the apostles' self-reproach, as if Christians are expiating this sin until the end of time.

But of all that, the disciples knew nothing. And apart from revelation they could not know it.

From the purely human point of view, however, there is no doubt that what they did was wrong. They left the right in all its unmistakeability to suffer outrage. They exposed their religion to extinction, their prophet to foul wrong and themselves to destruction. Nobody knows what would have happened to Christianity had they succeeded in rescuing him by force. But the fact remains that without doubt the line of action their reason had approved and the guidance deriving from their reflection and their intuitions were alike invalid.

If then the disciples, though the finest of men, were not saved from error after consultation and debate and having to hand all that makes for right guidance, the people of Israel have some excuse also if they proved to be misguided. They took the Christian religion for a piece of sedition, which would quickly have destroyed the pillars of their religion, their law and their nation. They supposed that the man was a sorcerer and his followers criminals. They proceeded upon purely human and self-made criteria and from human emotions in no way stamped with that ardent faith that characterised the disciples. If both groups, disciples and Jews, erred and went astray, what can anyone do in their desire to avoid error, as long as they proceed in what they do upon human reason alone?

To the present day, Christianity has not freed itself, and perhaps never will, from the entail of that sorrow and regret which haunted the souls of the disciples because of all that they were lacking in relationship to Christ at the time they held back from saving him. They have been destined to bear the reproach of the great sin – the sin of abandoning Christ to his foes, to his oppressors and persecutors. It seemed to them that they were only commanded to withhold themselves from rescuing their prophet because they did not deserve to be his witnesses.

And thus a dread of falling into sin, an apprehensiveness about evil-doing, has become a dominant feature of the Christian spirit. And so it will always remain. For Christians have no way of atoning for what happened on that day.

# The Disciples' Departure

❖

The disciples went forth from their place of meeting as the dawn broke and took their several ways into the city, spreading among their followers the news that the decision had been taken not to come to the rescue of their prophet, as long as to do so meant violence. They gave orders to them to remain quiet and peaceful and to renounce anger. They warned them against flouting their prophet's command, plain and unequivocal as it was. They agreed together to make their way to one of the villages of Galilee where they were to remain for some days until tidings reached them that would further determine their life and work. They were as despairing and grief-laden as ever men could be. They could hardly keep on their feet, so shattered were they by sorrow. Dismay gnawed at their hearts, and in their travail over all that had happened they scarcely knew whither they were going. In the intensity of their remorse, they lost the very power of rational thought, and went in the heaviness of their souls.

They knew that it was certainly right to have refrained from saving their master. He knew the right better than they. The wise man their friend had promised them that God would raise the master to Himself and bring him back to them, after some days. Yet in spite of all, the fact of Christ having so commanded them did not save them from being angry with themselves. Nor did the wise man's promise keep them from bitter remorse for their failure to do right by their religion. They were consumed with doubt lest this promise had only been given to them that their hearts might not be totally broken with grief and pain. In their despair they feared that God had forbidden them His mercy and withdrawn

His compassion, because of their wrongdoing. Each man fell to probing his innermost soul, his motives and deeds past and present, in order perhaps to discover some reason why the mercy of God was withheld from him.

Christians have inherited this rigorous sense of wrongness and sin. It has left on them an abiding impress, in the belief that every injury befalling any human soul is traceable to some sin he or she has committed, even if it was only in the realm of thought and of no serious significance. Such thoughts have continued to pervade Christian thinking. It has come to be one of the most characteristic features of faithful Christians to be dominated by fear of evil and to be apprehensive and dubious about any action involving moral compromise. And what actions are really free from compromising evils? Faithful Christians are more eager to avoid wrongdoing than to promote good. Their fear of wrong is more powerful than their concern for justice. Their dread of the fire of hell is greater than their effort to attain the garden of paradise. Furthermore they are more prone to prohibit the unlawful than to command the good. In their exhortation they enjoin abstention from evil more than admonition to good. Thus negativism overcame all their actions in times when Christianity was most given to worship and piety. Such characteristics tend to be natural to all religions, but they are most manifest in Christianity. It is strongly established in their creeds that a person is permeated with evil until cleansed, and it may well be that it goes back largely to what the disciples were made to do against their will on that fateful day.[16]

The knowledge that they were partners in the wrong and that their actions followed a line of communal consent did not save the disciples from self-reproach, because they saw themselves as individually responsible. People in communities take differing attitudes from those of individuals towards right and wrong and whether to act or not to act. Communities readily do the wrong because the individuals composing them share out the weight of guilt and none of them feels personally implicated. Each thinks of his partners as exempting him from implication in that his particular share of responsibility is very slight. He argues too that even if he had not participated it would have happened anyhow. Communities as such are not readily inclined to take action for the good, because the individuals who make them up prefer to have the credit. When, however, communities abstain from their obligations towards what is good that does not absolve individuals from reproach and pangs of conscience. For then each individual feels culpable, not having performed their proper duty, even though they are not alone in their disinclination and their reluctance for risks. So it comes about that as far as communities are concerned going forward to evil is easier and to good more difficult. Inaction vis-à-vis the good that should be done, however, brings a sense of reproach equally, whether it is at the door of a single individual or whether he has fellow defaulters. So the disciples when they left Jerusalem felt in a deep personal way the onus which that day lay upon Jews and Romans alike. It was as if each of them believed that had he delivered the master he would have delivered all the people from this act of sin. Each of them laboured under a burden of shame which lay heavily upon their shoulders and tormented their consciences. Expiation of their sins became their first pre-occupation and they felt an intensifying desire to atone individually for the sins of the people as a whole. Such atonement is one of the strongest pillars of the Christian faith. Even though passive action did not fit in with human predilections, at least it meant real obedience to God and its piety was the surest guarantee of being preserved from defiance against Him. One factor leading them to this conviction was the command that had been laid upon them.

As they made their way with heavy hearts along the road that led out of Jerusalem, there met them a large Roman convoy. At its head was a high and massive chariot in which rode a prominent Roman. He was short of stature, thin and puny looking almost to the point of emaciation. Behind came a contingent of powerful Roman soldiers and behind them a rabble of captives laden with chains. The convoy had climbed up to Jerusalem on its way to the coast, following a great victory in which the able men of the conquered territory had been made captive. They were bringing them to the galleys in which they would toil at the oars until they came to the immortal city, a cargo such as the soul of her people loved. Prisoners were that city's meat and drink, her delight and comfort and her proud array.

The hands of the captives were chafed with sores from the heavy chains which they had been carrying for days. It happened on the way that one of them became badly affected in the foot and was limping from weariness and pain. A guard nearby had been himself earlier a slave, in like case. For the Romans habitually choose the strongest of their slaves and subject them to the severest discipline until they become superlatively strong. Then they select guards from among them and pick out the best of them for wrestling matches, to the delectation of the girls and belles of Rome. These gladiators even kill each other. The toughest of men, their masters are the most effete. The guard in question came up and struck the limping slave with a whip. For a brief while he walked more vigorously. Then the effort overtaxed him. Hobbling feebly on both his feet, he began to upset the ordered movement of the line. Whereupon the whipping master came up and turned the whip on him. Unable to move on, he fell to the ground and when the guard raised him up he could not even stand. The movement of the procession was halted, to the commander's angry displeasure. His temper was the alarm of his Roman subordinates and they went to investigate what had impeded the march of the convoy. When the guard showed them the cause, they flew into a rage with him. No convoy headed by a great Roman commander such as theirs must ever be halted by such a petty incident. The guard had no success with his efforts to free the slave's hands from the chains which bound him to the others. With the officers growing restive he had only one recourse, to lop off the slave's hands. The poor wretch collapsed on the ground and the guard kicked him outside the ranks, as the convoy went on its way with two severed hands dangling from the chains. The Romans were delighted with this remarkable solution and with the presence of mind of the guard. They laughed among themselves as they returned, well satisfied, to the commander. That reassured the guard, dispelling his fear that perhaps this pestilential commander might be angry with him. For there was something terrifying about the fearful power he wielded.

The disciples were appalled and outraged by what they saw. Bursting with indignation one of them cried out: 'You people are foul criminals!' But none of the Romans heeded the speaker nor his remark. Had they noticed him at all, they would not have made sense of what he said. None of them thought that slaves were ill-served, any more than horses carrying heavy loads. They merely thought that slaves were made for such things. People were in no sense equal in their right to justice or mercy. The disciples went over to where the slave lay and tried to dress his wounds. But he expired in their arms and they buried him.

With hearts heavier than ever, they continued their way. For a brief time the incident they had witnessed took their thoughts from their own immediate circumstances. They got into discussion about it, their conversation revolving for the most part around the theme of suffering befalling the innocent. It seemed to them that religion cannot be a purely inward matter but is inevitably involved in the realm of men's relationships. The deed of shame done to the hapless slave greatly agitated their minds. To think that God, the source of all good, almighty, just and merciful, had allowed such barbarity to happen and that no heavenly retribution seized the perpetrators to prevent their action. They wrestled to reconcile the justice of God – since they had no right to attribute evil to God – with the actual evil occurring in the world. Two schools of thought emerged. One group alleged that what befell the slave and his fellows resulted, necessarily, from their being unbelievers and from sins they had committed. Had they been believers in the true faith this suffering would not have come on them. God is aware of the sins of men as no one else is. If suffering befalls an allegedly innocent person, this innocence is nothing more than our ignorance of his or her transgressions. To say otherwise is blasphemous unbelief, and errs from the proper confession of the transcendance that belongs to God. Is there not evidence of this truth in what actually happens? Can any of those who suffer boast that their faith is a true faith and that they have committed no sin? God would not have punished them so if they had been really guiltless. When evil befalls someone it is a speedy retribution in this life. As for those who reject God and do wrong and yet undergo no condign punishment here, it is only postponed until the world to come. Or it may be, alternatively, that God has in their case relented on account of some good they have done of which we are not aware. The majority of the disciples inclined favorably to this view of the matter, because of the degree to which it acknowledged sin and vindicated faith and lowly deference before God.

The other group found it in no way acceptable. They based their notion directly on what they saw, namely that injustice falls alike in this life upon both innocent and guilty. They considered it useless on our part to attribute to victims of suffering iniquities they had not committed, and to evildoers a repentance they knew nothing of and to ascribe it all to God. Those who adopt such views only bring both God and religion into doubt and disrepute. They could not accept the view that Divine retribution is visited in this life upon the defenceless only and that retribution for the rich and powerful is always postponed to the last day. They were not the only ones to be baffled by this question. We are perpetually puzzled when confronted with the problem of evil and the justice of God and how the two are to be reconciled.

To this perennial issue even the disciples found no solution for the believing mind. They dearly wanted to discover some answer which did not have to be explained with embarrassment. They fell back upon absolute faith, and on God's surpassing knowledge and our abysmal ignorance, beseeching God to grant them a guide who would show them the true reconciliation between the Divine justice and the fact of evil and the way whereby good could be wholly God's and evil wholly ours.

Actually this problem, so bewildering everywhere in every age, is not a matter that is totally inexplicable, if we were not misguided and if our knowledge of the laws of God as they relate to

His creation were not partial. The root of our mistakes is that we suppose ourselves created first and the whole world created later, and that, for our sakes, as if the principles of human life were first laid down and then, built on them, the laws of animal and plant life, of minerals and stars, to harmonise with the laws relating to humankind. But in fact, as is well known from the heavenly Books, humankind was the final creation of God. The world could subsist and proceed according to natural processes, whether humans had or had not been created. In actuality we are animals whom God created out of the dust, breathing into us what made us human. What He breathed into us was none other than conscience, the gift of God, possession of which distinguishes us from animals. It is part of our being as creatures. Without it, we would not be human. Reason, intelligence, speech, skill, are attributes of which the animals might conceivably have been capable had they attained a sufficient degree of progress, and without thereby becoming human. There are some who aver that conscience is our invention and not something belonging to our nature, since animals know nothing of it; as if one might argue that what is outside the realm of animality is an acquired capacity we have adopted. This is nonsensical. Conscience is just as proper to our nature as movement is to animals. Plants would have no right to argue that movement or fear are unnatural to animals because plants lack them. Without conscience, we would cease to be human. It is conscience which lays down for us principles of conduct of which animals are wholly ignorant.

Evil befalling humanity is of two kinds. One derives from our being animal – sickness and catastrophes due to the natural order. In these we are in no way different from the non-human. Harm besetting us in this sphere is no more an indication of wrong and injustice than the disease which may attack a flower or the sickness affecting an animal or the thunderbolt which strikes a tree, or the stone that hits a harmless pigeon. These are not injustices attributable to God. For God has not made His natural laws to depend on what is beneficial for us alone: they are more general and inclusive than that. Moreover, these laws are necessarily constant and are therefore operative whether or not someone quite undeserving of punishment happens to be involved in their effects.

The other kind of evil befalls us at the hands of our fellow humans. God has left this in our power and made us responsible for it. He has not constituted conscience a sort of tall fence, preventing us from trespassing beyond its limits. Nor has He made it a surrounding fire to burn up any one venturing through and beyond it. He has made it, rather, a guide and a mentor to be followed. But He did not make ineluctable punishment to turn upon transgression against it. The fact that conscience is part of our nature does not preclude this truth. Morality, religion and conscience, with us, are comparable to the role of water in the life of fish. They are indispensable to us. But we can transgress conscience, just as a fish can leave the water – and with the same result. Those who hold the notion that all this is not part of our nature but is a fabrication of certain people who seek to narrow our liberty, are grossly wrong in the way they understand things. The land animal would be wrong if it supposed that the fish's keeping to the water was a cruel restriction of its freedom or a deficiency in its brain, rather than something deriving from its proper nature.

It never happens that a stone falling to the ground is diverted from its course in order not to strike the head of a devout believer or an innocent child. For, as we know, such deviation from the laws of the natural order would destroy the whole pattern of things. Nor does the sword in the hand of some giant wrongdoer fail to cut off the hand of his victim merely because he is innocent. God does not frustrate the deeds of an intelligent person who is doing wrong or foster the doings of an ignorant and dull one merely because what he or she does is just and right. Those things do not happen. Moreover, they have nothing to do with the omnipotence and justice of God. Nor does the justice of God have any causal connection with the operation of natural laws in these realms. Had the popular notions of Divine justice in fact obtained, not a single natural law would have remained by which the orderly system of heaven and earth could have operated.

As for the evil that men and women bring upon one another, believing minds would like its retribution to be speedy and decisive, so that faith in God and conscience would be all the easier for people. But this too reveals an ignorance of the Divine law in the stuff of things as we know it. Only in the case of natural laws belonging to the inanimate world, like water flowing downwards, does the result follow immediately or inexorably from the antecedents. Animate creatures, however, are too intricately constituted for consequences to appear in the very wake of their antecedents. Life has a flexibility and a capacity for new contingencies. It has a complexity or knottiness in its laws which often results in a sort of hiatus between cause and effect. It also has the capacity to elude many consequences and thus their inevitability is far from clear. This non-immediacy of consequences increases the higher we proceed in the scale of living beings. It is greater with animals than it is with plants, and with us it is very wide indeed just because we are human. All this serves greatly to loosen the tie between good and its reward or evil and its retribution. The law of existence itself has not made that connection close or decisive. The intricacy of the laws of life – and that is the secret by virtue of which life is life – does not admit of their being applied in the way the laws of inanimate nature are. This situation in which we find ourselves in human life, whereby there is elasticity between what causes and what is caused, renders it difficult for us to identify the entail of any person's deeds. But all discussion on these questions of human existence leaves no room for doubt that those who follow conscience find within themselves increasing good, whereas those who transgress its limits become the locus of increasing evil.

It is for these reasons that the presence of evil and wrong in the world should not throw believers into confusion. It in no way justifies, as atheists suppose, any dubiety about the existence of God, nor yet doubts, as the faithful fear, about His almighty power or wisdom and justice.

The disciples reached their safe retreat and gave themselves to worship and prayer. The one burden of their petitions was that

God would not leave them to err and stray. Had they not been within two bows' length of going grievously astray?

They called upon God in these words:

'O God, Thou hast been gracious unto us and hast bestowed conscience upon us. It is a spirit from Thee. What it enjoins and what it prohibits are alike Thine. Whosoever obeys it, obeys Thee. The one who flouts it flouts Thee. Thou hast left to us the obeying of it. Keep our doings within the bounds of conscience. O God, do not let us be so encumbered with the things of this world that we transgress the bounds of conscience. O God, so inspire us that we follow no other guidance. Teach us not to override it for any alternative however impressive and to set up no idols to be worshipped or esteemed as good to its exclusion. For outside conscience there is no good. O God, guide those who preside over human affairs that they establish no order that will oblige others to transgress conscience and that they do not inflict on others wrongs that are immediate and concrete for the sake of something supposedly and ultimately good for society. For this is the origin of our tragic trouble and the source of the evil within us. O God, Thou hast endowed conscience with no material force to compel our reluctant obedience. So give us inwardly a spiritual compulsion in which we will follow it out of choice and delight. This will eliminate wrong, and the wiping out of evil and injustice will strengthen the faith of men and women and will guide them into the right path. O God, guide Thy servants who have gone almost irretrievably astray. Thou art the hearer and the answerer.'

# 5. Among the Romans

# A Resolute Commander

The Roman troops at Jerusalem were among the largest of imperial garrisons and the most illustrious. They were commanded by one of the bravest and most forceful of Roman officers. He held very familiar ideas about what befitted a Roman soldier and nothing was dearer to him in life than the glory of Rome and the might of her sons.

It was his opinion that Rome had not attained her greatness merely by unique physical strength nor yet by superb competence in the commanders of her armies. Her greatness derived from that veneration for law and discipline in which Romans were moulded and habituated. He prized discipline most jealously and this led him into extreme measures. He used to ferret out the mistakes of all who were under his command of whatever rank and kept careful watch on their lapses, which he visited with condign punishment. This attitude reflected no hardness in his nature. It was simply that he believed that hard discipline made the army more secure and was more conducive to victory, besides in the end economising bloodshed. For the sake of discipline, therefore, he was ready to deal harshly with a few. He considered that negligence led to defeat involving the death of many more soldiers than the imposition of discipline could possibly involve in suffering. He knew the troops did not love him but he believed he was performing his duty to the full and in that was his satisfaction.

It seemed to him one day, as he reflected, that discipline among his forces was no longer as strong as he wanted it to be. He sensed that there was some disorder creeping in among the younger men in the ranks, a group of whom were restless and insubordinate to their officers, even taking issue with them about the rightness of the orders they gave. A number also were in angry mood because they no longer enjoyed the varied pleasures they had anticipated and for the sake of which they were ready for soldiering. What he heard dismayed him. He determined to give his troops an object lesson they would never forget which would set them again on the right track, so that they would not dare ever after to take issue with him over what he did for the good and the glory of Rome. He imagined the whole life of the empire to be jeopardised if martial prowess slackened or if any tenderness and weakness became apparent in its actions. When such an idea gets hold of a commander, or a ruler or a judge, he loses his balanced judgement and falls into extreme measures.

They brought to him an adolescent boy, one of the youngest in his army, whose only crime was that he had stayed out after the time for turning in at night. When his officer interrogated him he shrugged his shoulders and turned away. When the officer rebuked him and repeated the question angrily, the soldier gave him an offensive answer. He was in fact drunk, a thing all armies regard as a violation of discipline which cannot be ignored. The commander decided on a court martial the following morning and gathered his leading officers and some ordinary soldiers to attend the court. It was an obvious case, the man having admitted what he had done. Those present remained silent, awaiting the commander's verdict. The sentence was that he should be given fifty strokes of the lash in the presence of the rest. All the company was astounded at the severity of this condemnation and the soldier himself went deadly pale. There was not one present but felt wildly indignant and a gasp went round the whole courtroom. The commander could have had no illusions about their being in no sympathy with his decree. But the fact only stiffened his determination and he resolved not to let their anger influence him to lighten the brutal sentence. The man had flouted discipline. Only one fellow got any satisfaction from it all – he whose job it was to do the flogging. His face told of a pleasurable anticipation he made no effort to conceal.

The soldier was bound with a rope to be flogged. The first stroke of the lash brought an immediate flow of blood. The victim's cry horrified even the commander himself. But he hardened himself against any thought of moderating the sentence. The future of martial valour and of Rome, not to mention his own future, depended upon his keeping doggedly to his course and paying no heed whatever to humanitarian sentiments.

The strokes continued until the wretched soldier's cries grew feeble. The bystanders thought he was dead. Jealous for every one of the allotted fifty lashes, the flogger stood over him. He wanted the tally full and exact. When it was ended, the man's comrades bore him away to a warm room, brought him wine and hot drink and tended him. He lay between life and death. The fellow with the lash showed no compunction when they accosted him. He had no regrets for his part in the affair. They expostulated with him in vehement and angry tones.

'You could have been less brutal and heartless: you're more callous than the commander himself. Even he showed some slight trace of compassion in his face. There was none on yours. What would you have done had he died under your strokes and we had then torn you limb from limb?'

'I used to think when I began this flogging business that it would be the death of many victims. But my experience is wider now. I've flogged hundreds and not one of them succumbed.'

'And are you sure that one of them one day won't kill you?'

'They are my best friends and I theirs! That is because after a flogging like this they all come to honour. It's this that makes them valiant men. Is it not the outstanding characteristic of victorious fighters that they can inflict wrong on others without the least provocation and kill them out of hatred and vindictiveness, without knowing them or being known and without there being any hostility between them? There is nothing that so fosters such feelings than for men themselves to be cruelly and unjustifiably victimised when they are young and tender. It is the lash which accounts for the emergence of most of our Roman heroes of battle. Those who are wronged do not come to hate the wrong they suffered or be resentful about it. Rather they develop a lust to oppress others and to inflict suffering on the innocent as a revenge for their earlier experiences. These are the best features of the men who win their fights: or at least so I have discovered in Rome's armies. When injustice is done to men, so it seems, their rational feelings for their fellow men give way to the passions of a beast of prey. This is the best apprenticeship to soldierly valour, as conquering generals understand it. You will see. This young fellow after his taste of brutal treatment will shortly be a man of exemplary bravery and honour.'

# The Traitor

Thus did matters go for a while in the Roman camp. The determined commander prospered in a most gratifying fashion and gained the commendation of his superiors in Rome. He began to fancy himself bye and bye as commander in chief in the ancient city. It would be a reward for his strenuous efforts and the vigour and keenness he had shown. Meanwhile, however, he was becoming increasingly aware of that group of younger men among his soldiers who, while not actually breaking discipline, were discrediting it and conforming to its demands only out of necessity. They were supercilious about the glory of Rome and referred to it contemptuously. They even propagated peace, alleging that a soldier ought to take under cognisance what he was ordered to do, scrutinise it critically and refuse obedience to what he did not find valid. These things vexed and enraged him mightily. Here, it seemed to him, was something utterly destructive of the military spirit. Such notions would rapidly lead to catastrophe and might well deprive him of the role of consul in Rome. He made up his mind to bring it to an end.

He had the idea that this corrupted mentality resulted from a prolonged absence from actual fighting. His army had become inured to ease and quiet. The best thing he could do to restore their ardour would be to throw them into warfare, into an action in which the issue was assured and victory could be safely assumed. Accordingly, he announced that the army would march on one of the border cities and take it. He found a trifling excuse to hand in the fact that one of the inhabitants had insulted the Emperor in the market of the city. Such an offence should not go unpunished, if it were not to recur. No one believed that this was the real reason for declaring war. But they were happy about it. A few thought that now they could find opportunity for the display of the prowess their officers were continually extolling in their ears. Most of them, however, were glad merely for the sake of the women and the booty they looked for when they conquered and plundered the city. They knew the captured city would be fair prey to them for several days before it became immune from plunder. They calculated what their gains might be. The leading officers were also glad about the venture, realising that extended peace corrupts the military quality of troops and engenders among them the sort of disgust and boredom in which insubordination and insurrection breed very readily. The glory to Rome when the campaign ended in triumph was a further attraction.

The commander prepared his forces with great skill. The hour of glory, he declared, had struck. This was their day of destiny. They would advance on the unsuspecting city and make short work of its inhabitants, teaching them to venerate and honour the immortal name of Rome.

The harangue followed familiar lines. His sentiments were exactly those of every one who before him had summoned men to war and urged them to hatred. Each, however, cherishes the notion that he is an original pioneer.

'Rome expects that every one of her sons will do his duty. There can be no doubt that you will fulfill this duty to your country, the fatherland whose skies overshadow you and whose earth has borne you, the land that nourishes us with its crops and refreshes us with the waters of its rivers. We must protect it against all who dare challenge it in word or deed. In so doing we defend our fathers, our mothers, our wives and our children; we protect them and make their name to be exalted among all as well as doing them proud in themselves. A number of you will be killed in the field and will be mourned by your families. But the field of honour is the field of immortality. If mothers fail to understand that is because they are women. You are men who set glory above life itself. In men cowardice is a shame that will cling to them for ever and earn them the scorn of all. War generates the virtues of bravery, loyalty, sacrifice and brotherhood among fighting men. It is ease and peace which make away with manliness. A man is no true man unless he hurls himself into the thick of the battle. If he dies he has won immortal honour: if he lives he is a gallant man of valour. By your death your nation will live. Its fate will be determined for centuries by what you do today on the field of conflict. Do not turn back upon your heels nor bring upon yourselves and your people the shame of disaster.[17] We die that our children may live in happiness and that Rome may become mistress of the world. Strike the people of the aggressive city such a blow that their descendants will never afterwards look upon a Roman soldier without trembling from fear.'

Impelled by his own enthusiasm, he went profusely on, orating about glory and sacrifice, courage and manly valour. He supposed, like all his counterparts, that his words would be the major spur to battle and that his eloquence had a magic power to inspire the soldiers to covet death for the noble cause. He imagined that the army would treasure his speech in their hearts and hold life cheap at the remembrance of it when the spears drew blood of theirs. It was his firm conviction that without this harangue not a man of them would have lifted a sword to fight nor braced himself to die.

The truth, however, was that the whole array was bored and wearied with his words. Not concealing their loathing for the speaker, they fell to whispering among themselves and grew increasingly restive, as if all they wanted was to be off. This the orator took for the high pitch of enthusiasm aroused in their hearts by his eloquent periods. He dismissed them convinced that victory, thanks to him, was already in the bag and that a splendid future lay before him, when Rome heard of the brilliant campaign and his triumphant personal part in it.

The group of malcontents, though few in number, were marching side by side and ridiculing all that had been said. They were not upbraiding the commander, whom they did not dislike, but were laughing and jesting as they exchanged remarks: 'It is a perverted logic this with which he glorifies war. We don't die in war that our children may live happily. It is he and his like who drive us their sons into it so that they may enjoy the pleasures of an easy life after we are stowed away in the ground. It only costs them a few tears shed for a few days while they remember us who die.'

Another said:

'Even odder was his claim that war is the source of all the virtues in those who fight. Has he not asked himself in whom these virtues come to be? Is it in those who die? But do you imagine that he has asked a single victim of war whether in fact the qualities of heroes were produced in him? Or are these virtues brought to pass in those who do not die? If so, then presumably we kill the bravest men in order to generate bravery in those who lack it? War only creates a counterfeit bravery in the likes of him, men who are far enough away from exposure to its perils. They are brave – but in our blood: they sacrifice – but our lives. Then we say they are courageous and self-sacrificing! Nothing makes me laugh more than this idea of admiring the courage of a man who commands his soldiers to fight to the death -- the death of every man jack of *them*. That's a proceeding that hardly calls for courage, unless perhaps in the sense that the commander must inure his feelings to the utmost pitilessness so as not to have any compassion for a single one of his men. Most of these commanding officers will escape anyhow in the end. And even if they are taken prisoner their victorious opposite numbers will treat them with respect. But no honour will be done to dead soldiers. It is true there are noble virtues in soldiers but they do not derive from warfare. Some peasants show artistic capacities but these cannot be credited to agriculture.'

Another said:

'If he really thinks that the death of hundreds of us is necessary for the glory of Rome, why is he not the first to die? Would he agree to our leaving him for the enemy to shoot at with their arrows so that one of him dies before hundreds of us do? If he were to do so we could warrant him then that we would fight like lions in his wake. If a man declaring war on an unsuspecting people knew certainly that he would die immediately the war began, nobody would ever have declared a war. Wars arise as a result of the miscalculation of men of state. There is no justice in the innocent, the learned, men of sound judgement and competence in the varied walks of national life having to die because of the wrongheadedness of some political leader, while he himself suffers in no way because of it. He who drives his people into war is a despicable gambler flinging the dice of other men's lives. He knows that if they triumph he gains the spoils and if they fail he is secure from all evil consequences. If you must have them, let there be wars, but they ought to begin with the killing of those who preach them.

'Talk about wars producing virtues in society at large also astounds me. It is a foolish and pernicious thing to say. The "community" in this respect is a fictitious idea not an actual reality. Virtues exist only in individuals. Wars kill off the bravest and most self-sacrificing people and leave the rest enjoying life without them.

'They say that nations cannot live without the glory of victory. That is a hollow lie. This superstitious delusion about glory ought to be totally destroyed. If there is glory in victory then there is necessarily disgrace in defeat. Which of the nations has enjoyed perpetual victory and glory? The days come round full circle. The peoples that are at one time in the full tide of victory are at another in the grip of defeat. What advantage is there then in one day gaining glory and on another coming into the throes of shame and dishonour?

'Otherwise, there is no glory in being victorious, nor shame in sustaining defeat. These things are nothing other than deceptions invented on behalf of vested interests, which the interested parties encourage the feeble-minded to perpetuate.

'Furthermore the only people who wax eloquent mouthing about this glory business are the very people who play no part in it. These are the living. But the dead, who really achieve it, do not speak of their courage and their sacrifice. This division of roles is grossly unfair, the dead in battle paying and the living talking.'

Another said:

'Militarism depends upon the circumstance that one man or

group of men wields more power than thousands of soldiers. That situation might be acceptable when the soldiers are a lot of ignoramuses of no worth or significance. But if the men in the ranks became an intelligent body of men what is to prevent them taking up a critical attitude towards wars? Would they then be willing to die for a notion in one man's mind, who certainly cannot be considered so much greater than they that he has the right to drive them to their death with contempt? The soldier with any education ought to be under no such authority at the hands of any commander. He should have the right to challenge the commander who orders him to advance and say: "Why should I?" If that were to happen the delusion of war would completely collapse.'

'All that would be true if war were always aggressive, like that to which we're marching now. But war in self-defence is an undoubted duty. Attack, too, may be the best form of defence.'

'That's what every aggressor says. In my view the test of aggression is whether the soldier is operating outside the frontiers of his own country. He who is outside the borders of his own land is the aggressor, whatever be the reasons for his being there.

'The leaders and commanding officers know that they have to deceive their people and make out that the aggression is really defence. It is a long-standing stratagem. But from now on nobody needs to be taken in by it. Another of their deceptive devices for the army is their claim that there are rules of war which mitigate its horrors and do away with many atrocities. But if you ask me, there is only one rule about war which ought to exist, namely that anyone going outside his own land to make war on a peaceful people in their own territory is the aggressor. These people have every right to consider themselves no longer bound in respect of him to any covenant or law and to deny him all mercy and clemency. He has no right to expect such from them as long as he is outside his own state killing and inflicting harm.'

'If all the nations were to outlaw aggression in this way it would mean the abolition of wars with all their horrors. But it would be highly dangerous for one single nation to adopt such ideas and thus become a solitary sacrifice for them.'

'No! such principles as these readily spread by their own appeal and it would not be long before they became general in all nations, if just one would take them up.'

It was the Christian soldier and his companions who talked of these things. The other soldiers were well content with a new campaign, indulging their hopes of victory, booty, plunder and prisoners.

The army arrived before the walls of the city and surrounded it. The Roman troops tried to scale the walls, but suffered casualties including a large number of dead. They withdrew for a few days but were again frustrated when they returned to the attack. This was repeated several times. At length, they realised that the city would not fall to frontal assault but would have to be surrounded, in order to cut off supplies from the population and compel their submission.

They sent troops to make a close inspection of the walls to ensure that there was no breach through which supplies could get into the city unbeknown to them. When they had reassured themselves on that score, they proceeded to prepare themselves for a long siege. They also set up patrols to go around the city walls every night to prevent the enemy taking them unawares in a surprise foray.

Behind the city there was a mountain protecting it on one side through which there was one narrow defile which led into the heart of the city. The citizens had barricaded it with stones so that their enemy would not be able to detect it, unless led there by some one who knew the secret. Provisions reached the city by way of this gap. The inhabitants were well aware that they had no chance of holding out against a long siege unless they had ample victuals coming in. This point of ingress was the only route. Accordingly they were desperately anxious that none of the Romans should hit upon it. Their men passed the provisions through by night out of the way of the Roman sentries.

It happened one night that a well laden convoy came up and

halted by the narrow passage. The people of the city started to unload the convoy's load, believing themselves safe from detection. They had deputed some of their soldiers to patrol the ground between the gap and the Roman forces, so that the operation could proceed unmolested. That night there were three Roman sentries on duty, one of whom was the Christian soldier. They were patrolling the walls of the city, according to their nightly practice. They had not encountered anybody in their beat. But after a while they spotted the convoy beside the gap and realised that this was where supplies were reaching the city. As they were drawing off with all speed to bring the news to their army of what they had seen, the city's sentries saw them and setting after them overtook them. Inevitably a sharp scuffle ensued, for the defenders knew that if the Roman army had word of this point of ingress for supplies, the city would certainly fall after a very brief siege. The outcome of the fight between the two patrols was a life and death matter for all the citizens. Two of the three Romans were killed and two of the defenders. Another defender was severely wounded, while the Christian Roman was unscathed. Had he made all speed to regain his battalion and give them the information about this secret access to the city, he would have become one of the heroes of Rome and victory would have been hers, with his all the consequent glory.

However, what he actually did was quite otherwise. He stood over the wounded sentry who momentarily expected to be slain. Romans, as is well known, show no mercy or tenderness to their foes. But when the sentry saw him bending over him and asking how he felt, he was reassured enough to answer:

'What do you want to do with me? Have you decided to cut off my head and take it to your people as a token of your gallantry?'

'I had no such idea. Rather I would like to know what you want. I might be able to lighten something of your pain.'

'All I wish is that you will leave me to myself. I have a mother, a wife and daughters: they need me for their breadwinner.'

'But you will die if you stay here. You cannot get back to your companions. Your leg is broken and blood will pour from your wound. You will succumb.'

'It cannot be helped.'

'I will carry you to your people: they are near: they'll take care of you. My own army is some distance from here: I cannot carry you there.'

'We never heard tell before now of such kindness. Can there be such human compassion in the Roman army? They are known everywhere for their extreme cruelty to their foes.'

'If you think it generous and manly that's up to you. All I know is, that's what I'm going to do with you.'

'Aren't you afraid that my side will do you some harm seeing that your return to your army must lead without doubt to the capture of the city, the death of the male population and the enslaving of its women folk? Perhaps my people will not permit you to return. At the moment you are a free agent. What makes you want to run the risk of becoming a prisoner by your own free choice?'

'If they do that to me as a return for what I do for you that won't be my responsibility!'

He carried the injured man to his people and explained to them his plight, committing him to their care. The citizens were amazed to see a Roman soldier carrying one of their own wounded home and fell to animated discussion among themselves as to what they should do with this remarkable soldier. One of them said:

'We cannot let him go back to his army after what he now knows about us. It is all a cunning trick, a remarkable one too, by which he has got to know everything he or his army need to know about us. If you let yourselves be taken in by this kindliness and allow him to go back to his people, he will return to you at the head of a conquering army. The sword will have you at its mercy. That's what you'll get for such remissness. There's nothing surprising in a Roman's deceiving you in this manner for the sake of the honours that accrue to victorious heroes.'

Another said:

'If his purpose had been to spy for his people he stood to gain nothing by carrying home our stricken sentry. He was already in possession, when he did so, of all the knowledge he needed. It would be the greatest crime to repay such evident goodness with other than good.'

When their decision was taken to leave him free to his own devices, they summoned him and said:

'We are not going to detain you in any way. You go back to your own lines. We are well aware that you have it in your power to ensure the capture of our city by your army. Ambition and fear may well be factors inducing you to do so, though then you would be repaying our goodness to you with evil. But we, for our part, have no desire to requite with evil the kindness you have done to us.'

When he departed from them, he felt happy about what he had done. Had not his first experiment in doing good just for its own sake brought him great reward of good? His heart was well content in the faith he had placed in the things he had heard and come to realise when he was with the disciples.

But he had forgotten one thing, namely that he had done what he did in defiant challenge to evil. The good in his action, great as it was, was not that utter goodness that is natural, not studied. It was in a sense artificial, because he had with set intent worked himself up to it ethically, much as people who are getting ready for a match or combat work themselves up to it physically. So what he had done was not the finest kind of goodness which is there only when the impulses come only from the pure essence of good.

The invading forces, thwarted in their objective of forcible conquest, grew restive as the siege wore on. After exchanges between the two sides, they made peace, on a basis that preserved the honour of both defenders and attackers. The two armies agreed that the people of the city should not molest the rear-guard of the Romans as they withdrew. They were also to bring presents, to abstain from allying with any enemy against Rome or abandoning any ally of Rome. Thus the Romans withdrew with an honourable peace, only that the commander was violently chagrined. He could in no sense enthuse over a Roman withdrawal from a city without accomplishing the intended objective. He bitterly resented the blow to Rome's prestige in what he could only regard as a damned reverse. The fact that his own dreamed-of honours had become the more remote only sharpened his passion.

The days passed and things returned to normal between Jerusalem and the other city. Frequent visits were exchanged between the people of the two territories and each became confident of the other's good intentions. The citizens began discussing with their friends among the Jews and Romans the case of that noble Roman soldier who had found a way of reconciling the virtues of compassion and human feeling with those of honour and loyalty. They took to lavishing praise on the Roman character which evoked such virtues in its people. They took it for granted that in talking that way they were celebrating Rome's fame and extolling her people. It came as a surprise to them to find that none of their Roman friends had ever heard such things in eulogy before.

It all caused the Romans considerable dismay. They saw nothing honourable in this action, nothing noble or good. Rather, in their view, it seemed an act of treachery to discipline and nation, an act of comfort to their foes. That soldier had deprived the nation of assured victory in a fit of weakness. For humane sentiments of this sort they had no admiration. Tender-heartedness befitted women better than Roman soldiers. When the commander learned the details of the story he was beside himself with rage. It was a simple matter to discover who the treacherous soldier was who had thus occasioned a Roman army's frustration. The commander had not the least hesitation about what he ought to do with a man who had ruined his personal hopes of highest eminence in Rome, and had brought failure upon Roman troops and loss of prestige. He determined to bring the guilty soldier to a fate of unparalleled severity.

He accumulated all the evidence against him so that there would be no possible room for doubt about his treachery, as a crime for which there could be neither palliative nor pleading.

That particular Friday was the day of the court's decision.

The commander passed a most restful night, confident that he would root out the foul pest and rescue the grandeur and honour of Rome. He fell to soliloquising:

'Order, discipline, is the finest thing life holds: indeed, it is the very secret of life. Thank my lucky stars I am master of this discipline, not its slave. It has set me in authority over men, not men over me, though it could just as easily be I that should be its victim. Discipline is the force that subdues the greatest men if they are under its authority: and it exalts the lowest men if they are its masters. It may rob of life itself numbers of those who lie under its authority. Yet for all that, it is a mysterious quantity, resting on precarious foundations of fear. It can very easily collapse and when it does so another system of discipline must replace it, and assume the same authority over men. Even highly civilised people in this respect behave very much like primitive people with their gods. The very animal they fear and tremble at the mention of, they worship bringing sacrifices and offerings, followed by clamorous feasts and ritual meals of which they partake. Then anon they adopt some other animal as god and offer comparable sacrifices to the new deity who is in turn massacred.

The soldiers may do the same with me and my kind. They hold me in awe for my valour and revere me as long as I represent discipline. It would be easy enough to kill us if they wanted to, or to make away with us in some tumult and revolt, supposing that thereby they would be liberating themselves from discipline in ridding themselves of those who represent it. But of course it will not be long before other rulers will arise among them and take over our role, oppressing them as we do. The new regime will be no less onerous for them than ours. But they do not appreciate this fact when they take their revenge on us. They do not realise that we are not so much the architects of the system as those upon whom it seizes. How can they come to see that to be rid of us is not to be rid of some regime or other. What really oppresses them is not those who represent it, but discipline itself. And from the thing there is no escape.

'I'm very puzzled. I don't know what to do with people.

'For my own part I'd prefer to treat them with justice and kindliness, in hope that discipline would suffer no loss of authority. Yet both mercy and severity alike fail to save discipline from popular insurrection. Mercy incites them against it and against its custodians and they soon rebel. Let that happen in my time and I'd be the first victim. Severity, however, only postpones popular rebellion against established order. The era of my people has lasted so long that men are on the point of rising against it. It appears to me that I had better put off their rebellion at least until I am through myself. The only way to do that is to make them more afraid than ever. Such intimidation can postpone insurrection against the system that dominates people, but by the same token it makes their ultimate revolt inevitable.

'I see no other way for it. The only choice open to me is to let discipline protect itself in its own way. The best means to this are repression and force. Though they will not prevent rebellion they will at least delay it until after my time. When I have got through safely the one who comes after me will have to reap the fruit of what I do. Compassion and justice merely enfeeble the order of things and bring about the complete destruction of discipline in no time. Furthermore, they imperil what is even more important than discipline itself, namely the principle of fear without which there can be no authority at all.

'But I have no business deliberating like this over my attitudes to discipline and order. A man on a tight rope over a deep chasm between two precipices is not well advised to spend his time discussing the rope, why it is there and he on it, and the purpose in view. All those things, if he lets himself ruminate on them, are likely to send him to his fall. There are some reformers of intellectualist type who think that people like themselves should be at the head of organised society, on the ground that it is better to have a man of parts in such a role than a man of no parts at all. The intelligence and wisdom of the man at the head of things they take to be a guarantee of justice and wellbeing. This is a mistaken notion, fit only for the intelligentsia. Men actually in power know that order rests on crushing force. Those who are in authority are in point of fact more in the grip of the system than the system is in theirs. They have very little power either to make the order more conducive to good, or to obviate the evils in it. If you have two men, one a dwarf and the other a giant, standing on the summit of a lofty mountain, they will both have the same view of what is below them. The capacity of the order of things both for good and for evil is tremendous; but the qualities of those in authority within it, whether good or bad, are of no moment at all. It is all the same whether rulers are sound or corrupt, just or tyrannical. As long as the system is one and the same the effects of their rule correspond very closely.

'What is it which obliges these powerful fighting men, and numerous too, to submit to my command? They fear me more than they fear death. Rather than defy me in my commands, they would prefer, any one of them, to throw himself beneath a horse and be trampled under its hoofs, or to face an elephant and be killed like he would kill a bird, or advance upon spears levelled at his breast and face them with admirable courage. The only thing that makes it so is that each of them prefers a death that is probable to a death that is certain. For I would mete out certain death to any who went counter to my orders or defied the authority of discipline – and the system and I in that sense are one – whereas when the soldier goes out to battle there is always a hope that he may escape death.

'It is this thought that they may return from war alive and the knowledge that the imperial order will never let any violator get away with his life which makes them risk their lives. They have each seen companies returning from battle, and each man cherishes the hope that he too will be among the survivors and that it will be their comrades who perish. But not one of them has ever seen a soldier flouting my authority and escaping death. Actually a soldier's bravery is really cowardice. It is I who make it appear to him to be heroism and sacrifice, while discipline persuades him that it is national pride and honour. Though his acceptance of authority is really stupidity, the system makes him consider it nobility. It is in fact the system's doing that his brothers in arms go out to face death, but I make it appear that it is brotherhood and loyalty. I adorn the whole thing for him in the guise of glorious ends and high prestige. He knows that I am lying even when pretending hypocritically to believe in what I say. He knows too that I can only put this across him because I have him in a cleft stick in that he is danger of death in battle, which is the lesser evil, or he will die at my hands – and from that evil there is no way out.

'We tell the soldiers that the coward who runs away from death with his fellow soldiers on the field of battle will find a lonely death at dawn with bandaged eyes. That, however, is really deception. Our slaying the coward is not a natural consequence of cowardice at all. It is the work of the order under which we operate, and quite unnatural at that. It proves nothing.

'The whole thing is very like what obtains between an employer and his workmen. As long as the employer has the power to dismiss them and, so doing, deprive them of subsistence, his mastery over them will be unlimited, even though their numbers run into thousands. However, if they concert together to take away this power then his tyranny over them will be largely impossible. All that will then remain of the system itself will be whatever is necessary for work itself. So it is with armies. If they were to rise up against their commanders and deny them the power to execute those refusing to fight, why then the major part of their power to tyrannise would evaporate. All that would then remain of the system of discipline would be what was necessary for self-defence. In that event none would fight except those who wanted war out of conviction or lust, and they are few.

'Those soldiers who fall in war boost my reputation greatly but get no kudos themselves. Chaps like us tell the troops that their name will live in glory beyond the grave. Yet I do not know of a single soldier whose name was mentioned after he was dead. Is it not the utmost hypocrisy for us to revere the 'unknown soldier'? That's a fine idea! and the biggest deception ever perpetrated in the name of any system of power. It will never harm any living person to exalt an unknown soldier, after he is dead, above kings and princes. Nor will it do the latter any harm to pay honour to a dead unknown. Maybe the fallen, unidentified soldier himself cares little about the honours paid to him. Living soldiers, however, nobody honours. It makes no difference whether they are fine, healthy men or miserable weaklings, they are given no prestige. They remain in their social station without ever rising out of it. Only the living talk about the glory of war, for they care nothing about the death of their fellows who are killed.

'I and the system – we remain supreme. I hold my lofty station on the corpses of dead soldiers. From time to time, maybe, it caused me disquiet that I owe my eminence to the corpses of men who died to exalt me. I am sometimes assailed by strange thoughts as if I sought to leave my rank and be in some humbler station where I would not be living with the stench of dead bodies – the inferior dead. But then I soon fall to laughing at these preposterous ideas. For if I did so I would expose myself to becoming a corpse like them, upon which some one else would climb to honour.

'Such is the system that shapes us. I am the first that profits by it. So let me hold on to it, whether it be oppressive or just, sensible or foolish, and let die who will die, in consequence of my sticking to it. It is the system alone that does men to death. It is I and my interests only that I advance by dint of it. As for those who die, they prefer the death to which they are driven by the system to turning and resisting it and taking the consequences. It all adds up in my favour. The brunt is on them, the blame on the system and to me is the glory.'

# Trial and Sentence
---❖---

It began in the early morning of Friday. The soldiers were brought out to witness, for it was to constitute a warning that no one ever afterward should dare to be the occasion of disgrace to one of the conquering armies of Rome.

They brought out also the accused. His company greeted his appearance in restless silence. How, they wondered, had he been carried away into committing such criminal treachery against his nation, knowing that there could be no other punishment but death? They knew their commander's harsh severity only too well. He would undoubtedly mete out the sternest punishment. They felt they wanted to stand up for him, yet the very gravity of the prisoner's offence left them no chance to defend him or indulge their wrath against what was coming.

Among the spectators was an Athenian, well versed in Greek philosophy, which however he considered over-intellectualist. It was wanting, he thought, because of the weakness implicit in its rational methods which admitted only rational demonstration. He heard that there was a higher wisdom in India, that Palestine boasted a significant religion and that Egypt enjoyed a rich science under an absolutist government. He formed the idea of visiting these lands to investigate the reports he had received of them and in hope that he might find the truth which had eluded him in the deficiencies of Greek thought. He had no final conception as to just what this weakness was. For he clung to the notion of his own Greek philosophers that truth was a specific entity attainable by the enquirer if he knew how to search rightly, a something which, when found, constituted indubitable certainty. Truth was for him a commodity a man might look for as one looked for gold. Men do not bother as to what precisely gold is or as to its existence. Their one and precise aim is to seek for it and produce it. Our philosopher's countrymen had much the same concept of our relation to truth.

They did not realise that while this might be a valid approach to truth relating to the mineral, vegetable and animal realms, truth as it related to humanity was a very complicated thing. For the individual is an essential element in the being of truth and it cannot be sought for purely objectively and independently of the person as a thinker, who is at once the artisan of truth and the seeker after it. Perhaps this is the most formidable thing the human mind has to face in seeking out the truth in those realms to which the mind alone relates, such as conscience, religion and moral life. This particular Athenian had been a while in Jerusalem and was conversant with what was happening there. He decided to witness this trial and then go at noon to the hilltop of Calvary to see what the Romans had made up their minds to do to implement the wishes of Jewry concerning the new prophet.

The commander appeared. He was well assured about his course of action and implacably resolved to stamp out the heresy which the soldier symbolised.

The prosecuting officer rose and said:

'I would rather the earth had opened and swallowed me than that I should stand as I do now to prosecute a Roman soldier for treachery. I would prefer the greatest disasters to befall Rome, even the loss of half her empire, than that there should be among her soldiers the shame of the betrayal of army and of nation.

'The soldier whom we judge today betrayed his nation and betrayed his army. His treachery brought about the defeat of an army well worthy of achieving resounding triumph. His treachery, moreover, meant that your fallen comrades have died with no compensating benefit to Rome, no sweets of victory, no crowning glory. They died as it were by his very hand, and those who sustained wounds, his was the hand that wounded them. But for his being a traitor only a few of you would have been killed and those few would have been immortalised in victory. The blood of your heroes would not then have flowed in vain. If the cause of his thus exposing his army to defeat had been that he shrank from danger, we would merely have requited him with our scorn. Or had he been cowardly and surrendered, his fate would have been that Rome disowned him and his people cast him out. Or had he committed some unpremeditated error or acted out of ignorance, with consequent denial of victory to you, we would have dutifully pleaded mercy for him. But he deliberately betrayed you and for the sake of his act of treachery he exposed himself to death. Indeed he showed unusual courage in committing his betrayal. This makes his case, in my view, all the more astounding. I tried my hardest to find out what it was that led him to this incredible course of action.

'I have heard him say that he does not believe in war or in the majesty of Caesar and Caesar's men. He sees in victory no glory and no honour. He seems to have forgotten that these are part of our very nature and have been from the time of the creation. It seems he doesn't know that the strong among men overcome the weak and that there's no having it otherwise. I have heard him say too that those whom he was ordered to fight were no enemies of his. He had no knowledge of them and they had done him no harm. Killing he holds to be legitimate only in the strictest self-defence. The valid reasons commanders have for making soldiers fight to kill and to be killed cannot, for him, be considered permissible. It amounts to the crime of killing the innocent. He has sundry other similarly fantastic notions which indicate a sick and deranged mind. It seems he wants to devalidate and so transform the whole constitution of the world.

'There can be no doubt his perversity has led him to ideas that directly threaten the overthrow of discipline and order and the destruction of the very bases of your army and the state. How this diabolical business had got into him was more than I understood. But while I was still investigating the cause of his derangement, I got to know — and what an awful discovery it was — that the secret of his treacherous conduct lies in a girl, a most degraded type of Jewess. The youth fell into her snares and she took him to a group of people whose only objective is to ruin

Rome and break the pillars of her empire. Their craftiness was too big for this fellow's head. They made out to him that it was a call to worldwide peace. They conjured up before him the picture of a humanity that had embraced the principles of peace and love, a human family living happily together and in no way preying upon each other, if only they would. But what really convinced him about what they said was this artful woman, a present day Delilah. He became her obedient slave, pandering to his lowest passions. It is on this account that he has betrayed both you and his people. It is this that makes me sure I should demand the utmost penalty against him. His crime does not admit of being forgiven. Were the ideas it involves allowed to spread, they would destroy us almost everywhere in the world. Our success derives from the wholesome fear we have created in men's hearts and to the awe in which they hold us. If once that prestige is lost our very slaves would massacre us.'

He proceeded to rehearse for the benefit of those present what the prisoner had done. None of them appreciated the real truth. None had the initiative, the thoughtfulness or the temper to enable him to understand anything about the principles the accused had espoused, and which he had imbibed from the disciples. They had not the remotest comprehension of them. Not a single one of them did the ideas stir out of his apathy. They merely wondered why any intelligent person could be moved by such principles into betraying his army and forestalling its certain victory. The bystanders were convinced of the enormity of his crimes. He undoubtedly deserved the utmost rigour of the law.

The prosecution went on:

'I had made up my mind that he should not be allowed to defend himself. For when was defence of treachery ever tolerated? But after ascertaining what I have discovered of his motivation I have concluded that his defending his notions would be the clearest evidence of his guilt. So let him proceed with his self-defence if he has any.'

And the soldier said:

'I was not aware that I had betrayed anyone at all. Can you

point to a single person whom I have betrayed? You will say that I betrayed those who died in vain before the walls of the city. But I am of the firm opinion that even had we gained the victory their deaths would still have been in vain. For what good have they brought us? They bring upon themselves death and upon their people orphandom and bereavement, and the same death, orphandom and bereavement to those who were living peaceably in their homes. No one either in Rome or in the besieged city benefits from that, except a small clique of people who were never in any personal danger or damage but who nevertheless subsequently enjoy all the pleasure and profit. Even the glory they talk so much about only attaches to a very few of the living. There might be some sense in the whole thing if it was the dead who had the glory given them and came to enjoy its fruits. But for those who fall to die in order that others who survive should bask in the glory is something I can neither comprehend nor approve.'

'Did I not tell you that he was possessed with a kind of madness which has made him rave like this? You see with your own eyes. But let him go on jibbering. You must be entirely convinced of his diabolical treachery and of the fact that he has done these things after long premeditation and from deliberate intent. He wants to change the very order of the world, putting you and the most worthless slaves on the same level.'

'Indeed we and the lowest slaves are one already in our enslavement to you. You are a master of slaves: you rob them of their liberty and their labour. And you, sir, take from us our life and the happiness of our people. Let nobody say that it is our duty to listen to our masters and our bosses in regard to wars. For they are the very ones who know least about what they are doing. According to what they say, they would have us believe that they have no desire for war. It happens only in spite of them. Then the incidence of war is a mistake of rulers. We should not have to pay with our blood the price of their ambitions and miscalculations and mismanagement, the price of their tortuousness of mind, their temperamental weaknesses and psychological disorders. We do not let them control our property for us without some outside check.

How shall we tolerate their being in absolute charge of our lives without surveillance? Would not that mean that living men were more vigilant about their property than about the lives of their brave, who die defending them? Do we not find great commanders preening themselves on their runaway victories the course of which turned on the sacrifice of the largest number of men? Was there not one who got the glory of having fought to the very last man he had and this was accounted bravery on his part? He knows he owes his high honours to other men's death and his good fame to the spirits of those who were under his command. Men in this position can be almost certain that if they are captured they will never be put to death, though in that contingency may be so covered with shame and fear as in the end to commit suicide.

'My brothers, I have not betrayed you, nor indeed any one. I have only betrayed wrongdoing and warmongering, and exploitation of weak folk like ourselves by the strong that they may wax ever stronger and their tyranny more oppressive. I have harmed none of you. I have only prevented you from killing a larger number of innocent citizens, whom you took for enemies though you know nothing of them. And I prevented them from killing a larger number of you and I frustrated your commanders in the pursuit of their cravings for further power and domination over you. If indeed they could possibly have greater power than they enjoy already. I see in that no treachery to anyone at all. The only reproach that could be laid against me was that I failed to aid and abet their oppression of the innocent and of you also, by which they perpetuate the power they have over you. In doing so I have rendered you a service inasmuch as I serve the cause of all humanity. If every attacking army were to meet with similar disappointment wars would be all abolished without doubt.'

The officers murmured that he had said more than ought to be allowed, and that his remarks might strike an answering chord in the souls of his brethren. But the commander permitted him to continue, telling them that what he had to say was as old as the first battle in the world. Thousands of thinkers had said as much before him and tens of thousands of reformers would say it after him and nobody would ever pay any heed even though it sounded plausible. Human nature and the power of the established order would never allow such notions to call to halt a single war, however strongly expressed. Nor would any soldier change his preference for possible death in battle to certain death through treachery. These ideas could no more stand in the path of the established order with all its imposing force than a man could stand up to a raging torrent bearing down rocks and stones. However courageous and sacrificial his attitude might be it could only end in certain death.

'They may say that war anyway is inevitable and that as long as it is so, words will not prevent it. They may add that it is treacherous for us to act like this in the time of battle, since these ideas will profit nobody unless they lead to the outlawing of wars. Otherwise, unilaterally followed, their only effect would be to weaken that one army in the war, thus ensuring that it would suffer heavy losses and have no possible chance of success. In that event victory would necessarily go to the aggressors, that is, to the real villains of the piece. This is a valid observation. But do you not see that ideas and principles, despite their weaknesses, have a force such as the sword does not possess? They alone are capable of overcoming the prevailing system which is too strong for a man to counter. I am putting forward these ideas as a prelude to attacks upon the systems by which people have gone astray. It may be they will penetrate your souls and fructify there, though that may only be so after a thousand years or more. Then it will come about that the fighting man will attain such a degree of mental development that will enable him to appreciate the extent to which wars are a deception practised on the ruled by the rulers. They will realise, too, that the individual's life is too precious to be sacrificed for some end you have imposed upon him.

'Eventually the youth of the world will stand together in one accord and say to their leaders: "There are limits you must not exceed and beyond which we will withhold obedience from you, namely matters of life and death. Otherwise we will obey you. It is not for you to say you are sincere, nor to invoke the general interest, and honour and national prestige as if these were absolutes. It is none of your business to sacrifice us for the sake of your ideas. They are all ignorant and wrong. And had they been sound and clear you have no right to go to the point of destroying us in order to carry them out."

'I will remind you of three prerequisites of peace. No war should be declared without consulting the opinions of the soldiers who will be killed in it. The soldier on joining the army shall swear not to go for any reason whatsoever beyond the frontiers of his mother country. Commanders must be absolutely forbidden to threaten the life of any soldier who resolves not to fight outside his own land. If you want to go further we can do what some of the inhabitants of that remote country did when they placed those responsible for declarations of war in a special domed building to confer together. If they finally decided on a declaration of war in the service of the nation, they crashed the dome down on top of them and went forth to war saying: "It's only right, this being the service of the nation, that the leaders should share in it equally with the soldiers." No war has been declared in that country since the population devised this procedure.'

At this point, the commander decided he had said more than enough. He announced that his treachery admitted of no doubt and that clemency in the case had become unthinkable.

It was the belief of those present that the young soldier was demented and that, however true and sincere his ideas might be, there was no means whatsoever of putting them into practice. The enemies were still quite unprepared to adopt them. The fate of any party, they thought, pursuing these principles, would be to perish at the hands of the strong. They were all prepared to hear him sentenced to death. Yet they were quite unready for the terrible shock of the actual judgement. The commander specified the manner of execution, namely that the prisoner's feet and hands were to be tied to four horses which would each drag him in a different direction. A silent horror fell on those present and the condemned man gave a shudder and almost collapsed to the ground.

The executioners began their preparation for carrying out the sentence. Four powerful horsemen appeared on the scene, men celebrated for their mighty exploits. They started cantering round the arena to exercise their mounts. Then they stood in the centre while the man's arms and legs were tied to the horses. Whips were plied upon their backs and they were ridden forward hard. In this way the body of the traitor was pulled limb from limb and fell upon the ground in pieces. The whole watching crowd was appalled by the fearful cry that went up. Some hid their faces fearing to look upon the scene. The most affected of all was the commander himself. He could not banish that cry from his mind nor get the spectacle out of his head. His thoughts gave him no peace and slight fits of madness ensued which grew on him as the days went by.

But at least men now knew the fate of traitors. They learned the difference between high courage and low treachery, between bravery and cowardice, between strength and weakness. For these were all there for them to learn in the contrast between this traitor overtaken by a diseased conscience and those four heroic horsemen who killed him. It was these last Rome held in high honour while they killed the innocent and struck terror into the hearts of all nations.

The people went off, each to his own customary daily job. Some were angry and outraged, others were well satisfied, endorsing what they had seen. But whatever their views, all talked about what had transpired that day. Yet it was not long before they settled down to their familiar lives and forgot the whole matter. It was as if this crushing injustice against the life of one of their number had changed nothing.

Some of the soldier's companions, men who shared many of his ideas, came to gather up his remains which were lying about in the broad arena where dogs had started to collect at the scent of shed blood. They would soon have devoured the sundered body had not these friends of the victim driven them off. Intercepted thus in the act of consuming their prey, the dogs barked furiously as they shied away. Some of them answered the calls of nature as they went and one of the watching soldiers remarked:

'Can there be human beings with no more capacity to hate wrong or yearn over justice than these dogs possess? Can it be that among those who have witnessed this murder are men who gloatingly enjoy its sweets as these dogs do? Are there those among the leaders of the nation who see in this innocent man's death no more than these wild animals see? After all he was only obeying his conscience: and he did well. If only the rest of us were to follow suit war would be abolished and people would live in security. He had the conviction that if a man is unable to prevent slaughter he should do his utmost not to let one side triumph over the other. Such a course of action harms no one except those who dream of victory. Those who exult in victory do very much what these dogs do. You see them gloating over the limbs of the innocent dead, gladdened by the fruits of victory they relish, and scenting them with delight. That is just how these greedy dogs see things. Is it right we should have among our leaders those who deck out this organised barbarism and tell people that killing a man for the sake of the victory of the community or the glory of the nation is an absolute duty, a point of honour for a brave man. For my part I regard the killing of a single person a crime that cannot be outweighed by a whole nation's glory, an empire's greatness and the delectation of the great of all the earth. The community is a human invention and has no conscience. Though what God created was the individual and though it is the individual who possesses the gift of conscience raising him above all the rest of creation, it is just the individual that the community disallows. To sacrifice the individual in the name of society is blasphemy against God and His holy law. Any system which proposes to do so is undoubtedly bad. Mount up, Rome, on the bodies of innocent victims, your own and others' sons! O ye who live, delight yourselves in the fruits of the death of your sons! Take your fill of pleasure in the system that allows the likes of you to kill pure souls like this one here. Enough for you the hypocrisy in your talk of sorrow for your dead and tender compassion for your wounded. You send them to their deaths only that you may go on pursuing your pleasures and because your passions are insatiable. Falsely you claim that in so doing you serve the community. It is merely the service of yourselves! Your deeds are your doom, while you chase this mirage of glory which you have made your gospel.'

# Pilate

Pilate, governor of the province of Jerusalem in those days, was a man of wisdom and perspicacity. He had picked up something of Greek philosophy and was a man of mental integrity. He had listened to the religious leaders of Israel, to the improvement of his soul. Some of their doctrines he had adopted and he was no stranger to the proprieties of sound conduct. A man of equable temper he did not run to extremes and had correct relations with those in authority among both Romans and Jews. He was, nevertheless, tenacious of Roman attitudes and of the severity and force in Roman character and had no mind to be lenient where harshness was preferable. He had no room for the softness of heart that might divert him from resolute handling of his subjects whenever that was required. On that particular Friday, though, he was oppressed in spirit. The Jews had prevailed upon him to yield to their demands for the death of a man about whom he knew nothing but good. He realised full well that they were in the wrong and that he was himself. But in a matter on which they had their own point of view over an issue that was purely their concern, he had not thought it his business to counter them. Nor had he wished to give them any opening to accuse him in matters of his governorship. He did not see that he should allow his love of justice to jeopardise his authority and expose it to sedition, the ill effects of which would recoil upon himself. So he had been obliged to yield to their demands. But he was angry with them and ill at ease with himself. How he detested them for the deep disquiet which afflicted him, all occasioned by their obstinate perversity!

Pilate had a shrewd and accurate opinion about his military

commander. What he admired about him was his singleminded enthusiasm for the discharge of what he believed to be his duty. True he had a narrow mind and limited intellectual resources and opportunities, with no literary or philosophical education. But these aspects of the man did not detract from Pilate's esteem of him. He knew well enough that the greatness of Roman arms rested solely on the toughness, strength and valour of those who bore them. A certain measure of stupidity and lack of refinement might, in fact, be regarded as necessary for the development of these qualities. Intelligence, knowledge and high-souled character can easily undermine the characteristics befitting the combatant soldier.

A messenger from the garrison came to him with tidings of what had happened that morning and of the trial and execution of the traitor. He informed Pilate that the commander had returned to his house in a high fever and was now in a state of delirium. Many, he added, conjectured that what he had done with the soldier was the cause of the sudden onset of fever. Others ventured the idea that he was only experiencing the sort of fever soldiers catch when they wage warfare in marshy swamps, so there was no connection with his being conscience-stricken or troubled in spirit.

While Pilate pondered in his palace on the trials and tribulations that afflict the lives of rulers and the wrongdoing and callousness required of them, his friend the Greek philosopher arrived and the two began to talk.

'You have heard what the army commander did today? He knew of one of his soldiers who was guilty of treason and sentenced him to death. Sentence was duly executed. It does not concern me whether his decision in the case was right or wrong. But he chose a dastardly method of killing which makes it clear that he was incredibly angry and mighty ferocious. A modicum of philosophy would have obviated that. It would have been enough to put a bit of compassion into him and put a brake on his spirit. Then what he had in mind would have been rightly performed.'

'Give me a rest from this philosophy of yours. It has been borne in upon me today that we men of action can find no value in philosophy when any really serious issue confronts us. Philosophy in its own realm is a fine thing, but when matters drive us hard we derive no guidance or direction from it.[18] If the practical man wants to benefit from the wisdom of the thinkers numerous difficulties nevertheless arise. They attach to the inevitable business of moving from the language of thought to that of action. It is an exacting thing to translate verbal directives into the actions they indicate. This is because philosophy rests upon the definition of things and the judgement of philosophers about them is a deduction from such definition. But the practical man does not know how to define what he is doing until he has done it. For this reason philosophy has failed to guide rulers in what is right. Courage, for example, in your book, is the mean between bravado and cowardice. This is true and incontrovertible. But I and my military commander do not know whether what we have each done today ought to be considered rashness or cowardice or bravery. Philosophy leaves us with no indication as to the truth about what we have done. It offers no sure guidance by which to determine the question, except when the deed is done. Most philosophical judgements on events are analytical. What men of authority have to do with is not analytical but pragmatic. For that reason your guidance has been very feeble indeed as far as we are concerned.

'Nor are the men of religion any better guides, for us in the life of action, than you are. What they have traditionally to say about truth and error, good and evil, is fine talk so long as it remains tradition, creed and faith. But it all becomes vague and ambiguous when the time for action arrives. Don't you realise that the Jews, most meticulous as they are in following the doctrines of their estimable faith, yet consider the lighting of a candle on the sabbath a heinous crime. Crucifying the preacher of this new gospel, however, is duty positively enjoined by loyalty to religion and nation! Men of religion, when they tender us advice, do not distinguish between the less and the more important. Things with them are either approved, or *verboten*. On their principles, there is nothing to help us in choosing between two legitimates or in discriminating between two *verbotens*, when one of them is unavoidable.

'Our virtues have to do with civil life, yours with intellectual, those of the Jews with religious life. I have become convinced that there is no feasible reconciliation between them. So let us order our affairs in accordance with what seems right and valid to us. I know what is good in our case. But trying to be guided by your standards or criteria will only bring upon us utter confusion of mind, a restlessness of soul and an irresolute will.'

'I have no desire to discuss the crime for which this soldier was killed, nor to question whether the verdict against him was just or unjust. But I would have liked not to find you so outrageously harsh. I would your men had more heart than to tear people limb from limb in this fashion, irrespective of whether they actually do so in the pursuit of justice and regardless of the nature of offence committed. If a verdict is a just one a sense of mercy in no way detracts from the force of justice, while if the judgement is unjust, mercy lightens the weight of injustice.'

'This that you call outrageous is not what bothers me. What bothers me is how I am to know what justice is and follow it, to know what is unjust and shun it. Compassion in unjust rulers is like humanitarianism in war. Both are really a piece of hypocrisy practised on people so that injustice and war cease to trouble their conscience. How can it be logically valid to deny a person all justice and then be merciful in the way you murder him? Or to compel a man into battle to fall there and then be taken with pity for him when he is only wounded? Does not all this simply come from our desire to mitigate the burden of injustice and war in human life? Is it not wholly hypocritical, a subterfuge by which the living deceive themselves lest their own consciences should rebel against them? What I want is simply a means to prevent me from wronging those I govern. If I see no light on this, it is all the same to me whether in oppression and war I am compassionate or savage in heart.'

'What you are asking for is guidance from philosophy and from reason, in a limited fashion, in respect of the actual problems you encounter in the exercise of authority. I do not consider that is possible. The things of life, of reason and religion, are more knotty than to admit of being ordered as simply as that. The assessment of what is right in life is more intricate than can be determined by such simple criteria. The latter are themselves always varied and sometimes also contradictory. That does not mean that philosophy has nothing to offer when practical men consult it for direction. Philosophy energises the mind for authentic thinking and strengthens its capacities as a source of guidance, so that when the time for action comes the individual judges more validly and has a greater feel for justice in his point of view. Philosophy is a mental discipline that prepares the mind for right action. Its effect in that sense is greater than what it can achieve by way of specifically defining what the action should be.'

'All that you say gives me no assurance that philosophy is a real guide to truth. Philosophy no doubt tones up all the qualities of the mind, both good and bad, with the result correspondingly good or bad, with the bad mostly predominating. Men of religion have an advantage over you intellectuals in that they do sincerely want to guide people and define precisely what should not be done.'

'I do not deny that they have this desire for people's guidance. But I do reproach them for certain aspects of their pattern of thought. They accumulate many things that have nothing to do with the principles of religion. For they lack any real exercise in the ideal method, the principles of which are clearly shown in philosophical thought where it is carefully mapped out. They talk of things for which they can offer no evidence and lay down vast hypotheses without adequate premisses. The biggest of these is the postulate of the existence of God which is the solution of all problems. But as far as we are concerned it remains hypothetical. Moreover, they confuse creed and knowledge, mistaking dogma for sound perception. They confuse also the eternal and the temporal and give to what should be confined to religion a role in matters that are purely rational. Furthermore, they defend the social systems they believe to be good on religious grounds. But such systems change perpetually and it is intellectually invalid to tie them to religion, which is eternally constant.'

'Do you imagine that your most stable sciences rest on other than unproven hypotheses? The best and most assured of your sciences is geometry. But the whole of it was constructed by Euclid on a hypothesis for which he offered no evidence, namely that parallel lines never meet. Without proving this, he contented himself by saying that if two parallel lines met they would not be parallel. And on this flimsy basis stands the science you consider most secure of them all. Don't you see that this foundation is as frail as a spider's web? It is indeed a childish hypothesis if compared with that first great presupposition of religion – the existence of God. For the latter has an origin rooted in human consciousness and our intuitive feeling is an evident ground of its validity such as scientific hypotheses by no means possess. You may say the hypothesis underlying geometry is established by the soundness of the results, and the numerous truths which, with such fertility, it validates, and because of which it can hardly be built upon what is false. But the hypothesis of the Divine existence is also an exceedingly fruitful one. Indeed it is the source of everything good and beautiful and admirable in humanity. Surely this renders its validity as a hypothesis entirely incontrovertible.'

'I do not reproach them for the proposition that God exists, but for their confusion between the things of faith and the things of action.'

'I heard from Caiaphas that religious leaders have a duty to the empty spaces in people's souls – those who have had no chance to cultivate their minds. In supplying religiously what such people lack intellectually, religious leadership implies no strictures on reason in what pertains to its role and where it can carry the burden alone.'

'And that, on their part, is precisely the source of a very great problem under which people will be groaning for long centuries. It is this compulsion to differentiate between things rational and things religious. Caiaphas and his kind have got confused between them in adopting this idea. It will be called the problem of reason and religion. It has no other origin but this mistake in their thinking. It is all very confusing and we must get out of it if we want the truth.'

'I see that you persist in talking about getting to the knowledge of the truth. I have no wish to divert you from your search. But what I am after is guidance. I used to think I had reached it by the way of religion, or religion and reason. But what the people of Israel have done today in the name of religion has destroyed every vestige of my hope for guidance there. From now on I shall seek it no more. I will remain a simple Roman soldier doing what is enjoined on me by the principles and traditions of my nation and by the consensus to which Rome has come.'[19]

'But why all this despair? Life, reason, religion — all these are arenas of the human spirit, all true, all beautiful and all exhilarating, though, of course, complete harmony of their respective demands is impossible. If hitherto nobody has been able to bring them into unity, they nevertheless represent humanity in its most progressive aspects. It may be that the centuries to come will achieve what we in ours have been unable to accomplish.'

'That is a beautiful dream, which I hope will come true. I used to dream it once. But today I am not as I was yesterday. Be clear about what I say: I tell you I strove hard to find guidance and I failed. I no longer see clearly any way to it. But you — well, you have no other concern but the search for truth. I only hope you won't end up in the same disappointment and despondency that are now my lot.'

The philosopher realised that in yielding to Jewry Pilate had brought upon himself a great tragedy. That crossing of his Rubicon had brought him to despair. Henceforth there was nothing for it but to follow the Roman philosophy and live for life's pleasures. No more had he confidence in the power of religion: he would no longer believe in the capacity of reason to guide humankind.

He went out immediately to the mount of Calvary, to see the climax of this matter that had brought his companion to the point of repudiating everything in which he had believed. He reached the hilltop a little while before noon.

Shortly after, darkness enveloped the world.

# 6. Golgotha and After

# Darkness Over All the Land

❖

It was noon time and the sky was clear. Then thick clouds rolled up from every direction in a few minutes. Deep shadows enveloped Jerusalem and it grew so dark that a man could hardly see his outstretched hand in front of him. Hail fell and violent winds lashed the city, uprooting trees. Jerusalem had never known such an event at that time of the year. None could remember having witnessed a tempest like it except a few very aged folk who said, as old people are very likely to do, that they had seen such a storm once before.

For three hours the whole land lay darkened.

Those three hours seemed like an unending age as fear and agitation filled people's hearts. All were profoundly disturbed at what the darkness might portend. The people of Israel knew that before now God had brought nations to destruction in just such wind and darkness. They thought the hour was at hand and passed in mental review the transgressions they had committed which were worthy of being visited by the Divine wrath. They remembered too that when no such retribution for their evil ways had befallen them they had gone on further into iniquity, thinking the Divine requital still a long way off. Now they were sure the great day of accounting was upon them.

In vain did the Roman troops try to play down the import of the strange event. They told people they knew of a distant country where such darkness frequently occurred. It was indeed quite a familiar phenomenon to them: in no sense did they regard it as a warning of punishment nor one of the signs of the 'hour,' though they had no notion as to what the 'hour' was. The Romans took to laughing and to ridiculing the craven-hearted sort who sensed danger in everything — people who promptly lose their sleep, taking every natural occurrence as an ominous portent, as if the only reason for all the mysteries of the world was to arouse alarm in their souls.

In point of fact people fall into two groups whenever they are suddenly confronted with a natural event, the reach and range of which they do not understand. One group, the minority, is neither disturbed nor dismayed and takes no evasive action. The other group registers profound dismay. These are the majority. The respective attitudes are not to be traced back to bravery or cowardice. They are natural to us when we have to face the untoward and the unknown. It is a very different matter from our reaction to known danger. The bravest and most courageous of us in warfare may be the most fainthearted when pitch darkness or unknown peril besets us. This fact is very apparent in the case of small children. Even among the very smallest you will find the one who has no fear when he or she encounters something strange and unknown, whereas a brother or sister is completely terrified. Yet both are tiny children and the reaction in neither case is a matter of rational cognisance. People observed such things frequently among their children when there were air raids during the last war.

The storm raged with winds of increasing violence. Frightened by the sound of the elements the populace of Jerusalem kept indoors. The streets were left deserted. The darkness was most intense over the hill of Calvary. On the summit of the hill, at the place called Golgotha, namely the place of a skull, stood a little cluster of people. There were a few Roman soldiers who had been jesting and chattering before the darkness fell. There too was a small company of godly women, believers in Christ, who had come to see their master and prophet before he took his departure from this world to another. There also was a citizen of Jerusalem, intent on all that had to do with his religion, who had come to see the end of the heresy and to witness the destruction of the conspirator and his lawless movement.[20] That very morning he had been arguing with the wounded merchant and had left his house in anger over this faction of unbelievers. There also was the remaining Wise Man on whom God had bestowed knowledge in unique measure. He had left the disciples on their way to Galilee and had come to watch the setting of the star by whose light he had been guided to Bethlehem some thirty odd years before. There also was the Greek philosopher and that little shepherdess with her flock. She was the most distressed of all at the sudden darkness and cried out bitterly. When bystanders guided by her shouts went over to where she stood to find out what was the matter she was on the verge of tears.

Nearest to her was the Greek philosopher, who asked her why she wept. She told him that in that darkness she would never be able to make her way back to her tent and that her father would beat her for not returning home before sunset. She was in no way reassured when he told her that the darkness was not because of night having fallen. 'In that case, said she, this is the darkness my mother used to tell me about. When I had disobeyed her in anything, she used to tell me that the evil spirits would come after me and take me off in black darkness to the land where they dwelt. I often disobeyed her and nothing like that ever happened. So I came to the conclusion that what she said was just an idle threat with nothing to it. But here, sure enough, is that very darkness she spoke of and the jinns are going to take me away and I'll never come back.'

When the Roman soldiers who had also come up heard this story they laughed at her childish simplicity, insisting that they were very familiar with darkness like that. It would very soon disperse and they would all go back to their homes as safe and sound as could be.

The believing women came up to the little girl who was still trembling with fright. When she realised they were there she felt much more composed than she had felt with the strange men. They quietened her fears, assuring her that the darkness had nothing to do with jinns, nor with her being disobedient to her mother's wishes and that no harm would befall her. The cause of the darkness they were certain, intuitively certain, was the foul wrong done against the holy apostle who that day had been condemned. They had no doubt that God had called natural phenomena into service that people might take warning and desist from evil. If that were not what lay behind what had happened how would anybody be henceforth restrained from flouting moral laws? This was the Divine way of things, the path by which God preserved at least some measure of rectitude, honesty and true dealing among humanity.

The Jew who was with them assumed that he had acted rightly in resisting the new heresy with stern force. He was glad that he personally would witness the last end. When darkness enveloped the scene he became very agitated and distressed. Knowing full well that he had been a strong advocate with others of the violent persecution of the new prophet, charging him with falsehood, he said within himself: 'I am one of the evil doers whose retribution God wills; He has sent this darkness to warn them. How great is that prophet when God sends down thunderbolts on men because they have done him such wrong. The people of Israel slew prophets before now and no such marvel as this was sent down to them as a sign.' He began to think again about the prophet. There could be no denying that he was superior to all the prophets of Israel. A new found faith took possession of his heart and he regretted that he had not had a better and wiser judgement at an earlier stage.

The Roman soldiery, however, made no attempt to probe the significance of the darkness. For them it was merely a cloud covering the sun. There was no point in their searching for any underlying meaning in it.

The Wise Man, however, and the Greek philosopher listened to all that was said, the latter questioning the former as to his opinion about the darkness. They fell to debating it and as the exchange between them lengthened the darkness took on growing significance.

The learned Magus said:
'There is one thing about the events of this day of which I am

aware which you do not know. It is that God has raised the Lord Christ to Himself. He was the light of God upon the earth. The people of Jerusalem would have nothing to do with him except to extinguish the light. Whereupon God has darkened the world around them. This darkness is a sign from God to show that God has forbidden them the light of faith and the guidance of conscience.'

'All that is poetry and symbol, having no real relation to the truth. Moreover, there is no proof of it.'

'What truth do you mean? What evidence do you expect? Do you want me to present you with some individual man or group of men, deprive them of belief and conscience and so have darkness come down upon them? Do you refuse to be convinced except by that sort of evidence?'

'What I am after is that everyone should have proof of the validity of what they believe, a proof that their point of view is right. Nobody is on any account going to tell me that truth is relative or in flux, or that there is truth unsubstantiated by evidence. That is intellectual anarchy. It leads inevitably to a state of affairs where superstition, reason and religion are all on the same footing. You are postulating the presence of an immaterial factor in the occurrence of this darkness, whereas it is in fact a purely material phenomenon. One could only conclude otherwise if a purely material explanation was insufficient to elucidate the source and cause of what occurred. This unhappy shepherdess here also assumes another immaterial factor. But for my part I stick to rational criteria and on that basis there is, I know, something more in your idea than hers. However I do not want to believe what is mistaken.'[21]

'My first concern is that you should have a real faith, whether what you believe in is right or wrong. Faith is that intuitive faculty by means of which we are able to recognise the underlying significance of what goes on around us, and the implication of what happens. If you recognised some relationship between the material realm and what is beyond it, you would qualify as a believer. For believers and unbelievers, one may roughly say, are two different types of humanity, irrespective of what the believer holds or the unbeliever denies.'

'For my part I see no connection between abstract ideas and things material. I am unable to understand rationally how an act of unbelief can be a reason for clouds coming in the sky.'

'To believe in the actuality of anything does not depend on understanding its essence and its truth intellectually. You have no right to deny what you cannot intellectually conceive. Don't you see there is causation linking lightning, thunder and torrential rain, even if we do not understand what it is. Superstition may give us an erroneous explanation. And science too may explain it wrongly, or maybe rightly, or again the origin of the entire phenomenon may elude us completely. But at least there can be no doubt that some causation does exist.

'How the ideal operates on the material is in some measure known to us. Take for example shyness. It is a wholly immaterial thing. But it brings into the cheeks blushes and these are of course a thoroughly material phenomenon, occurring whenever there is shyness, and in other circumstance too, like fever, and sometimes from purely natural factors. The material explanation suffices. But if we accepted your logic we would also have to deny any connection between bashfulness and reddening of the cheeks. Bashfulness, it is true, is a result of education and habit and these have a quite remote connection with the dilation of blood vessels in the face. If you were to try to convince a girl accustomed to being naked that nakedness caused a psychological state in the modest girls of our race which led to reddening of the cheeks, she would consider it a matter merely of feeling and metaphor, not as something really actual.

'Is it not possible that the immaterial and the material alike are the result of one common quality, just as thunder, lightning and rain result from one common situation? Do you find it completely impossible to conceive of clouds gathering and a storm brewing and breaking, all as a result of Christ's being raised to heaven, in the same way that the rising of blood to the cheeks derives from a girl's development and education? The denial of intangible factors in the material realm would disqualify us from understanding the most important elements in the truth about it.'

'But my believing in the existence of some link between the raising of Christ to heaven and the onset of this darkness adds nothing to my knowledge that the darkness is a fact. Really I do not see, therefore, that your idea about such a connection is any better than the notion of this ignorant little girl, so long as you do not allow reason to be the arbiter. I know of no other criterion between what is false and what is valid. I see that you do not admit its authority in matters of faith nor have you established any alternative authority. You take refuge in the symbolic to explain actuality and it is just this proneness to believe in symbol that tends to grow more and more extravagant. If we were to give free rein to our imagination to conjure up connections between phenomena as it pleased, then chaos would become general and truth would be lost.'

'All that I want you to believe is that there are forces at work in our lives whose essential nature we do not understand, and cannot understand, unless the beast offered in sacrifice to God is capable of understanding that devotion, piety and atonement for the sins of those who sacrifice it, are the cause of its being slain.

'If you believe in the presence of this powerful immaterial element and its influence in our lives, you have, in my view, a more robust faith than that of those who merely believe in the traditional fashion. However, the determination of what is right and wrong in the content of our belief is a matter involving those who believe and no one else, assessing it by the standards of the belief itself. Were faith to come into your heart it would be a ready matter for you to recognise the right and the wrong in what you believed. Faith loses nothing of its virtue by the fact that it is reposed in the wrong thing.'

'You surely realise that the ultimate form of comprehension in animals is intuitive, and since mind transcends intuition, an animal, by intuition, cannot conceive what reason is nor understand its inner nature. Likewise with us: our highest capacity in understanding is mind or reason and when faith transcends reason we, by our reason, are incapable of conceiving what faith is and of understanding its essential nature.'

'But who, may I ask, set faith above reason?'

'The answer is clear enough. Faith can only subsist in intelligent beings. Reason, however, is found in believing and unbelieving people. It naturally follows that faith is above reason, though this does not mean that the former supersedes the latter. But it indicates at least that faith may have an authority of which reason is incapable.'

'All that only makes things obscurer than ever. Don't you see that what has happened today before our eyes, namely the crucifixion and the descent of this darkness, are specific events and the truth about them must be clear and specific too, and it must be one truth about them both.'

'How can that be so? If you were to ask every single witness of these events, each one would give you the whole reliable truth with entire assurance. And it would differ from the whole reliable truth which every other would tell you with equal assurance. If you were to ask these particles of stones and their atoms what had happened today, they would tell you that absolutely nothing had occurred. For the laws belonging to particles and atoms do not allow them any knowledge of darkness or death when these eventuate. Were these entities to affirm that nothing had happened, that would be the whole truth. If they reported otherwise it would be either imaginary or false.

'If you were to ask the leaves of the tree about the darkness they would tell you of it, because they are affected by light and darkness, though they know nothing of the reason for it. Had you asked them about the crucifixion they would have averred that nothing had taken place, for they have no comprehension of the laws of the animal world. In such reporting would be the entire and reliable truth.

'If you were to ask the sheep, they would tell you that this darkness is the night. For to them that is what this situation customarily is. Had you asked a sheep about those crucified it would have said that they had died, when they were hanging, just as brother sheep of theirs before had died, when they were hung up. And they would regard what had happened to the dead as a very familiar death, being unable to see in it anything else. For they have no knowledge of retribution and injustice, which within their experience have no part in what is real.

'If you were to ask the Roman soldiers about the darkness, their idea would be that it was merely a natural occurrence. Had you asked them about the crosses they would have told you that they were a punishment for crimes which the crucified had committed, namely two brigands and a leader of national insurrection. They understand crime and punishment, but have no comprehension of atonement and redemption.

'Do not on any account let your scientific instinct and your intellectual powers lead you astray here, or you will see in these events no more than these soldiers, though you have a far sounder intelligence and a more penetrating vision. Of course undoubtedly your ideas are closer to the truth than those of these ignorant fellows. But ignorance, knowledge and intelligence are not the only elements in thought determining the individual's capacities in arriving at the truth and in formulating what it is. These believing women and myself, and this little girl of a shepherdess too, have an innate feeling that obliges us to seek out the inner significance of what has happened and the underlying implications of these occurrences. We may be right and we may be wrong: we may be your inferiors in everything to do with reason. Nevertheless our capacity to sense the underlying meanings endows us with a strength you do not possess. You cannot pass upon what we believe in. It is uniquely ours and we have taken its measure by means of faith alone.'

'You seem, then, to be claiming that truth is at the mercy of the particular capacities of its assessors and their susceptibility to the various laws of their status, whether it be natural, animal or human. That idea does not correspond to any valid school of thought. It is neither intelligent nor scientific. It is a notion I have never come across in any of the philosophical schools with which I have had to do.'

'Schools of philosophy judge truth by what they have come to understand. It is a mistaken habit of rationalists to incline always towards negating things.

'A still more serious error is that you do not want people to believe in God until they understand His attributes rationally. You do not wish them to be guided by anything until they are entirely clear as to all that the guidance is. This is a surprising attitude on your part. It is like wanting people not to employ fire to warm themselves until they know its nature, and not to follow light as a guide until they know what light is, and not to make use of boats until they understand the law of Archimedes. Is not this preposterous? Do you think the mariner who looks at the skies and says, "today there will be a storm, I will not set sail", is to be considered in error because he has no proof of what he says? He founds his life upon his experience, and human experience is valid evidence in purely human affairs. We believers say to intellectualists: Let people be guided by God and do not deny them this guidance before they understand rationally the nature of the relationship between God and themselves. Do not cast doubt into their minds about intangible things pending the time when they will rationally appreciate the connection that exists between things intangible and things material. Do not forbid them the moral virtues until they can understand the essence of how they are related to the laws of life as we see these operating in the animal world. There are some intellectuals who deny everything that is uniquely human, because they do not consider anything natural unless it is reproduced in the animal world. That is a claim that is patently false. It might well be likened to the idea of some tree that all movement of animals was unnatural because it had no parallel in the plant world. One of humanity's most characteristic features is the sense of the supernatural and our faith in it. It is precisely in this particular that we are above the animal world. The fact that animals have no knowledge of what is mental and are not under its aegis is no reason whatever for our denying the realm of the intangible. Perhaps when the Taurah said of Adam that he was the first man, it did not mean that he was the first being to walk on two legs, but rather that he was the first to become aware of sin and to feel the influence of conscience. It was in this that he became human. This is the spirit of God which He breathed into him so that by His grace the man became capable of faith and also of becoming God's viceregent upon earth. This is the most characteristic attribute of humanity.'

'If you had limited faith to the acceptance of the fact of things intangible, of conscience and of God, we would not have found that very difficult. But you want us to concede some connection between things superhuman and things sub-human. You aver there is a causal connection between the nature of the moon and the stars and the nature of conscience and things moral. All that derives from faith and in your view faith is only complete when there is this bringing together of the material and the ideal, of what belongs to reason and what belongs to conscience.'

'Perhaps it was Moses, upon whom be peace, who began all that. For so pure-souled was he that he addressed his conscience in plain terms and without ambiguity. The truth of what transcends the human was revealed to him in a way that no other human being had experienced before him. But he was not only a prophet. He was also a learned man and a ruler. His powerful mind led him to see that there was a relation between this sublime truth and wisdom and the laws upon which humankind must proceed. He came to the conviction that God was the sole source of that relation. Nor did his reason find any flaw in that conviction. The fire and smoke, the steam and the explosion with its rumbling thunder, and the molten metals in all their variety as he saw them, were to him the common issue of the one origin, namely fire. He summoned men and women to faith in God Who is the source of all we see in existence.'

'I see you are reverting once again to symbol and simile, both of which are of limited range in the clarification of truth. We involve ourselves in error if we make undue use of them.'

'There is nothing reprehensible about thinking with symbols. It is indeed the only way people have whereby they can express for themselves and for others the meanings that lie beyond the senses.'

'I am still as far as I can be from an understanding of the truth about what happened in our presence today.'

'You cannot blame yourself for that. Today's events will remain the theme of debate for very many centuries. People will be perpetually contending over how to understand the truth of them and their implications. Two parties will persist – one of belief and the other of disbelief – sharply at issue. You are by no means the only one who cannot understand it.'

The philosopher began to see that even in the simplest matters it is a very difficult business to know the truth. He had just the same feelings of despair that had overtaken Pilate in the realisation that truth and right guidance alike were hard to come by. In his distress of spirit he was sorely grieved to discover that his effort after truth had been no more than the pursuit of a mirage which his mind had pictured for him. In actual fact there was no such thing as truth of the sort he had been seeking.

Little by little the darkness began to lift until the sun reappeared and was soon shining again as it had been in the forenoon. The sun's return was greeted by everyone with joy. The little shepherdess hurried after her sheep and hastily made her way homewards, delighted that the jinns had not snatched her away while everything was dark. She made up her mind to pay little attention to her family's threats.

The three hours were ended and each of the bystanders had exactly the same set of beliefs, unchanged and unrevised. The 'sign' had altered nothing in their several attitudes. The sceptic remained sceptical; the believer held to his faith; the ignorant were as ignorant as ever. The Wise Man still held to his view that the darkness was related to conscience. The believing women persisted in their faith that the darkness derived from the dark deeds of the Jews against the prophet. The Romans were still sure that it was all part of nature, while the philosopher took the dispersal of the darkness to preclude its having any explanation in evil deeds. For these last remained, whereas the darkness had gone. The shepherdess was still dubious about jinns seizing her one day. None had changed his convictions, save the Jew, who had come to witness the destruction of the heresy. He now believed that the new religion was neither heretical nor seditious, and returned to his home a believer in the Lord Christ.

Thus the signs of God avail only those who are ready in soul for the impact of things religious. He was by nature a believing person, and it was a comparatively simple matter for him to move from one belief, and that mistaken, to another, and valid, faith. But where the individual is not disposed to believe, signs make no impression. We see that the signs of God belong only to those who are naturally people of faith and whose souls are receptive to religious emotions and a sense of the 'world invisible.'[22]

# Return to the Sermon on the Mount

❖

The Wise Man hastened to Galilee to meet the disciples where he had promised them. When he came upon them shortly before sundown, he found them at worship and prayer, though they hardly knew what they were doing. For they were in the utmost grief and despair. The foul evil they had witnessed on the way had only sharpened their anguish of spirit. And then there was that darkness that had covered the city. It was hardly calculated to lighten the burden of their souls or to bring any solace to men who had abandoned Christ to be the victim of the malice of those who cared nothing.

He greeted them and said:

'How is it that you are still so broken hearted with sorrow? If you are grieving on his account, well, God has taken him to Himself. That is something quite beyond doubt. Before long tidings of him will be reaching you. If you are sorrowing because of having been guilty of a failure in duty, know that he has forgiven you everything because of your obedience and for the fact that, by holding to the call of peace, you have not contravened the dictates of religion. Know that God has given you the lowly commission to preach the new religion. If you are heavy of heart out of fear that this religion will die out now that it is left to you, know that in your hands, and in the hands of those who come after you, it will spread until it reaches the uttermost part of the earth. If you continue to be so despairing you will be too weak to perform your sacred duty and so your disobedience would be greater and more serious.

'The Lord Christ bids you go out far and wide into the world calling men to the religion he has taught you. For this mission you must draw from him the heavenly power of which you are so sorely in need. You need, moreover, the guiding wisdom to teach you the proper way of accomplishing that on which you are setting forth. You will find the fullest guidance in the sermon on the mount. It is your business to take it in authentically and to trust it, fulfilling its behests more worthily than the generality of men and women. For with the majority of believers the sermon will remain a lofty ideal. Only a few will be of mind actually to fulfil what it says. People will plead excuses to evade its commands when they find them onerous. The fact is that God knows well their weaknesses and has lightened their burden.[23] Had they all been as pure-souled as I see you to be He would have held them to patterns of behaviour closer to His guidance and would have enjoined on them more exacting and rigorous laws. But it is your duty to see that your faith is deeper and stronger than is incumbent on humanity in general. It is your duty to understand the sermon rightly and to follow its teachings in all their sublimity. In responding to its call, do not be satisfied with what you are temperamentally capable of. You remember the day when you and I and my brethren heard that sermon on the mountain side for the first time. When we returned to our own land we scrutinised and studied it with the utmost care. Its warnings and exhortations became clear to us. I want to talk to you today about the things to which our study of it led.

The law commands you not to kill: the sermon commands you not to be angry. For anger evokes hatred and evil leads to murder and injury. It is your business to teach people that he who compels a man to kill other men has killed both him and them. Murder and the inflicting of injury can never be good. No aim can justify them, however noble it be. People will say that killing is legitimate when it is a matter of terminating rebellion and corruption. But you must understand that only God and His apostles know how to identify sedition and corruption for what they are. It is not for someone who has no inspired status to judge whether there is an occasion of lawless defiance of truth that calls for killing. Nobody has such superiority over another that he can justifiably put him to death. Nor has anyone adequate wisdom or knowledge of the unseen to warrant him requiring people to die for some idea of his.

'People will claim that killing and inflicting injury are lawful sometimes on the plea of the defence of religion, and the protection of creed, and at other times on the ground of the defence of the nation or of themselves. Be warned against both. He who bears arms or harms people in the name of the defence of religion sets religion above God, Who has ordained love, not murder. God is responsible for the preservation of His religion and is in no need of sinning servants to save it. Nobody has attained such a state of infallibility as to make his ideas about credal deviations so valid and inerrant as to legitimatise killing. Those who defend religion by persecuting others only defend their own notions. Indeed the majority do no more than defend their own rights and privileges, and merely adopt the plea of defending the true faith as an excuse.

'As for defending the fatherland against its enemies by aggression, this too is a vain folly foisted upon men by frustrated people who are strangers to good. Had they more wisdom they would have spared their people having to die for mistakes of their committing. He who sends his people into war kills his own before he kills his enemies. Both combatants suppose that their adversary is the aggressor. Each side believes it is they who are acting in self-defence and for the preservation of their fatherland. This is a fantasy by which men deceive them — men who are either without conscience and restraint or who are plain criminals and ignorant. Killing provokes retaliation and one of the parties involved is bound to be defeated. But the evil consequences are indivisible and constitute something which both share. The defeated party bears of course the evil done, while the victor develops an incapacity to act justly. Tyrannising over the enemy, he comes to lust more strongly after tyranny and in the wake of victory falls to oppressing his own people. You never find a nation that oppresses its enemies and continues just to its own people. He who wants to have justice repossess his rulers, let him prevent them from becoming accustomed to tyrannising over their foes, or those they think to be their foes. Self-defence is only legitimate for an individual in the case of outright direct aggression against him. But the claim of general aggression against a nation or country is a vain assertion that does not justify involving men in total slaughter, as we see it in war.

'God alone has the right to deprive us of life or to involve us in injury to ourselves. We have no right to bring about the death or suffering of anyone on any ground whatsoever. For such things are an infringement of the prerogatives which are God's alone. Since we have no ability to restore life to our brother, once it is taken, or renew him in health when his health has been undermined, we have no business jeopardising life and health at all. Whoever does so, trespasses against God and arrogates to himself a knowledge and wisdom that God alone possesses.

'The sermon has made plain to you the nature of the kingdom of heaven. It tells you that the kingdom belongs to the poor and the simple-hearted, to the sorrowful and the humble, to those who strive after truth, to the merciful and the pure in heart, to the preachers of peace. It is your task to show the way of the kingdom of heaven to those who are contrary in their character, to the rich, the sagacious and the mighty. Poverty and simplicity find their virtue only in spiritual purity. Riches excite unruly passions: power and intelligence bring the temptation to oppress. Prosperity destroys purity of heart because of the patterns of life to which, for the sake of it, people submit themselves – patterns which are imperfect and harmful. Those among the rich, the intellectually gifted and the strong, who are able to maintain a purity of spirit are, from the standpoint of the kingdom of heaven, poor without poverty and simple without simplicity. They truly become secure members of it. For it is not wealth or intelligence of themselves which prevent anyone from entering the kingdom of heaven. The crucial thing is purity of heart and of conscience.

'The law says to you: Do not commit adultery. The sermon warns you that whoever looks upon a woman lustfully has committed adultery. There are those who think that this sin of adultery is the only form of immorality and that all the evils in the world belong derivatively to God's punishment upon illicit relations between men and women and that the greatest sin is sexual lust. But you should know and teach that it is only a sample of unruly passion, which religions have taken as an example, because it has such over-mastering power and because anyone who can hold its impulses in check can likewise restrain other passions too. What God has made unlawful in regard to sex is meant to exemplify the truth that God has outlawed every unruly desire that incites us to violate the rights of others. These other lusts and passions include ones that are more far-reaching and injurious even than sexual evils and more productive of mortal threat to the life and security of society. For the human conscience rejects an anarchy of desires, equally, whether it relates to sex, or property or prestige. It is erroneous to tell people that the prohibition of adultery is for the preservation of blood relationships and the protection of the family. The social mores could change and these things no longer constitute a restraining sanction. At all events, the prohibition of adultery goes much deeper than that. Furthermore, I warn you: Do not be over given to concentrating all immorality in this realm of sexual desire. For some people will then suppose that all other passions are permissible and in that case you would cause them to miss the true significance of the proscription of adultery. For the law intended the outlawing of every mastering lust. Teach them that anyone who looks upon any possession belonging to someone else and who longs after it with the sort of desire that makes him plan to do someone harm in order to gain it, has in fact committed adultery.

'It was said to the people of old: Love your neighbours and hate your enemies. The sermon tells you to love your enemies and bless those who persecute you. But, much more than that, you should know that you should be people who have no enemies at all. Enmity only exists among us when our desire after what belongs to others intensifies and we want to lay forcible hands upon it. What we for the most part covet has nothing to do with happiness or well being. Most of the jealousies among us concern

# Golgotha and After

food to eat, clothes to wear, luxury in all its self-advertisement and the acquisitive power of the wealth of those who are rich. And none of these are any indication of happiness. Plates of gold do not help the appetite, nor silken clothes ensure good health. They hardly deserve to be sought at the price of enmity, hatred and envy. If only people learned to enjoy the beauty around them and their own endowments of health and vigour and the good in their souls, the poor would not bear malice toward the rich. Hostility, ill-will and envy are not natural to us. They arise from our incapacity to appreciate the beauty in life and from the assumption that the good is always what somebody else has, as well as from the misdirection of social relations.

'All the sacred laws have forbidden the worship of idols and the instinct to deify what is not God. They made it the foremost transgression and the most serious of offences. But if the intent of this outlawing of idolatry had merely been that people should not worship stones, religions would not have given it such attention, nor would they have identified it as the great enormity. For the time when people worship stones passes away of itself, when they emerge from their first barbaric state. The day is soon coming when there will be nobody on the face of the earth who thinks of worshipping a stone or an animal. Reason is sufficient in itself to indicate that stones are not to be worshipped or have offerings made to them. The sacred laws would have dispensed with all this emphasis on the outlawing of idolatrous worship and "association" with God, if the whole matter had been merely concerned with images and their worship. What the laws were after was the prohibition of something vastly more serious, something which is in fact the root of all evils.

'Know, then, and teach people that there are idols they worship which are neither stones nor statues. They can make to themselves idols which are in no way stone entities. Yet, worshipping them to the exclusion of God, they become involved in far more grievous wrong than the sin of outward idolatry. They will call these idols "principles," and lavish on them a greater veneration than that accorded to conscience, offering their very lives upon altars of sacrifice in the name of principles. These idols will turn people away from true directions of life to a quite terrifying degree, such will be the impotence of their consciences, the perversity of their minds and the corruption of their reason, all in devotion to idols worshipped in despite of conscience. Every time an object of worship of their making is destroyed, they fashion another. They discard the first and scorn those who worshipped it before their time. Among these idols to which men and women will bring their allegiance are national prestige, nationalism, loyalty, freedom, obedience to authority, the law. These they will call the civic virtues. And there will be other idols too dubbed virtuous also, such as courage, sacrifice and the general welfare. They will be sticklers for the acknowledgement of prosperity and dominance as things sacrosanct. Indeed, the worship of idols will reach such a pitch among them that they will kill themselves in order to defend the flags of the army or state frontiers or royal honour. All these things are popular gods. They may be harmless indulgences unless and until they conflict directly with conscience or the Divine command. When that happens, however, to bow to them and to worship them, in defiance of conscience is atheism, idolatry and gross error, even if the guilt of actual image-worship is not involved. He who worships religion itself in such a way as to transgress the bounds of conscience and wrongs others on the plea of defending religion is truly guilty of having another god in God's place. They are in gross error who think or believe that the community is greater than the individual, or that communal interests have priority over personal, or that society's gain can rightly be had by ignoring individual conscience. The concept of 'society' is an idol which you are invited to worship by people who promote it only in their own interest and delude you into thinking that society can prosper when its individual members do not. That is an idle legend on the lips of people who really mean that a whole lot of people can be wretched for the sake of the happiness of a few. The general good is the most dangerous and injurious of idols, when worship of it rides rough shod over the dictates of conscience.

'Tell the world: Do not be deceived by the words of those who preach these principles to you and would delude you into thinking that they intend only your good. If what they stand for contradicts your conscience, you are under no obligation to obey them. To do so is plainly the way of error.

'The command of the sacred law is: Do not steal. Now people are not usually over-given to thieving. But in actual fact, everybody who makes profit for which he has not really worked is stealing, even though his method of doing so is recognised by law as permissible. Anyone who gains possession of anything by his wits and shrewdness, without putting anything into it, but rather defrauding the person who has, he is a thief. The sermon assures you that you cannot worship two gods nor reconcile the worship of God with the worship of mammon.

'It is your business to make people realise that the best way in which to worship God is to love one another. The Mosaic law laid greater stress on justice than it did on love. Recognising that people are incapable of this love, of themselves, you must lead them into mutual love of one another in God. For that is the secret of true piety and the source of all good. No one will ever find a more satisfying experience all his life long, a satisfaction untinged with regret or sorrow, than making possible another's happiness. Such a one will never have reason for the remorse that awaits those who wreak harm on others in the pursuit of fleeting prosperity or passing whims. The secret of happiness is to confer happiness on others, and this can only be by love. The call to religion among earth's peoples is an exacting task for you. I have no fear for religion because of what has occurred today. My fear rather has to do with you and with those who will bear the burden of the Gospel after you, and with the encounter between religion and daily life and with the issues that obtain between it and human reason when the latter is assertive and confident.

'I am also apprehensive about your enthusiasm to bring people into faith in this religion, lest you fail to keep the whole and the details in perspective, or to distinguish the root and the branches, between what is religion proper and what is just wisdom or valid opinion. Eternal truth must be carefully distinguished from temporal good, as well as what belongs essentially to human nature and what derives from man-made systems. The potential confusions here will trouble both you and those whom you call to the faith.

'My view is that you should build your mission on three principles of religion, which you will never fail to observe. These are: that you should not worship idols, in any of their forms; that you love one another; and that you shun all unruly passions that flout conscience. These three fundamentals: faith, love and restraint, are what – as being of the nature of religion – you must summon people to in your preaching. Anything beyond that, preach only on the ground of its being wisdom or valid thought. These, namely wisdom and sound opinion, may change. Let your concept of the scope of religion be broad so that it will not be difficult for people to keep within it and leave them freedom of action in their daily situations, letting religion mean inclusive commands and prohibitions of significance. That is more conducive to their being held in proper reverence.

'I am afraid lest you go too far in giving religion a loftiness of ideal beyond the reach of people's natural endowment, so that they do not follow it. It is your duty to make it acceptable by everyone who is naturally capable of belief. Another danger gives me pause, namely that your religion stands as you see it upon beliefs that only mystics accept and upon principles only understood by the best of people, on ethical standards feasible only for the simple, the poor and the ascetically minded. The day will come when mystics will be few and nobody will appreciate the beliefs involved, when eminently good people will become scarce and no one will comprehend these principles, when simplicity and asceticism being rare their moral values will go by default.

'So talk to people in a way they understand and do not use excessive symbolism. That may suit noble souls and the "natural believers". But keep in mind that your fine language with all its splendid wealth and range of imagery and its power of imaginative description can even make the symbol seem the real and the imaginary actual. It can flow along with its own full momentum and has ponderous capacities. But by contrast, the languages in which you will be preaching the new religion are precise and incisive. There things are not taken allegorically. If, for example, you talk to Greek philosophers about a vital force in people urging them to evil and driving them to mutual injury, and about there being conscience in the human constitution, about conscience restraining this vital force from over-mastering them to their own destruction, or about conscience being the source of all good and the innate urge the source of evil – all such things a Greek philosopher, addressed in those terms, would understand properly. And possibly after that he might take to you with some confidence and understand something of acts of worship and prayer, of things outlawed and of sin. But if you were to throw all these things at him without such precautions in your terminology, you would get a cool and suspicious reception, because of the contrasted patterns of thinking between him and you.

'I fear the effect upon this religion – indeed, upon all religions – of time, progress and intellectual advance. Religion is *sub specie aeternitatis* and it is your duty not to subordinate it to what is within the competence of reason. For intellectual advances bring changes in our understanding of things. But it is not appropriate that religion should change with them, lest it should thereby lose its sanctity.

'Let none of you on any account summon others to the active following of religion on the ground of its being good, in a worldly sense, to do so. For if you do that you will give people a loophole for the complete repudiation of religion, if they come to think that adherence to its precepts exposes them to danger or forbids them the pleasures of life. Rather, invite them into it on the ground of faith as something inseparable from being human, as that without which a person is no more than an animal.

'People will demand of you that religion should be an instrument to curb injustice. They will require of you to be staunch and vigilant against tyrants and oppressors and to give people a system that will destroy evil. But that is not the business of religion. For religion has to do with conscience, and society as such has no conscience. Religion can only influence the social and political order indirectly. It influences communities insofar as it influences individuals. If every individual were eager not to flout the directives of his or her conscience that would render evil impossible on the part of individuals in the mass and on the part of communities. And in that event, it would be a matter of indifference whether the system as such was good or bad, old or new. For religion to try to substitute one system for another is not its work. The new order itself would soon be in need of change. Systems come to be, flourish strongly and pass away, for reasons outside religion and beyond the control of the individual. If religion were itself to set up some system of life which people then saw fit to abandon for another one, that would do away with respect for religion and with the will of men and women to submit to it, even in its most intimately religious precepts.

'Social systems are in perpetual flux and change and necessarily so. But religion is constant. So the two are quite distinct entities and ought not to be regarded as interdependent. I and my brethren have studied the factors that make for untruth among people. We have located them in the worship of idols, in violent acquisitiveness and in the rejection of love. We may well achieve little in trying to direct people to the good in detailed terms. It may be more efficacious if we teach them faith and love and self-discipline, leaving to their own intelligence the organisation of their affairs within the limits that conscience allows.'

Many of his remarks bore upon matters with which the disciples were quite unfamiliar. They had still no actual experience of preaching the Gospel and were altogether unversed in its difficulties and the methods by which they might successfully go about it. All that they had understood of their religion had to do with the soul and with the individual. As the nature of the task ahead of them became clear to their minds they revived. A joyful hope pervaded them. They realised that a long enterprise lay before them, in which they would find deliverance from their grief and regret, from the shame of their weakness and the bitterness of their collapse. They were confident that this was the true mission, the *jihad* which would harm none and bless all. They resolved therein to offer to humanity an example without precedent in history. They went out far and wide with the message of truth.

# Conclusion

If humankind ever learned any lessons, they could find a wealth of them in the events of that day. But people never heed. They would have realised how the people of Jerusalem had quite evidently violated the truth, in this fierce encounter between the contrary forces of good and of evil, in which evil had overwhelmed the good and the true way had been worsted by the false. Truly they knew not what they did. Humanity is still in the throes of those forces and people still wander in error, as did the nations of old. They still prove incapable of confronting their temptations with any assurance of emerging uncompromised by false choices.

There are three forces at work in human life: the vital force with its instincts, desires and strivings; the power of reason with its competence to know; and the faculty of conscience with its conception of right and wrong. Each of these has potential for both good and evil. The good in physical life lies in its providing the incentive for action and stimulates to effort and exertion. It is thus the source of activity, and without it all bodily and spiritual functions would come to an end. However, its evil side lies in its vehemence and masterfulness, and in the fact that it is a blind force with no purpose save the perpetuation of life. It never reaches beyond that and it knows no direction or self-restraint. Reason benefits people by the light it sheds upon life's ways. It gives them knowledge and enlarges their experience and their capacities as well as their skill. It has its evil aspects, however, in that it is liable to deception and tends to make rationalists believe it is ultimate and absolute. Conscience, though, is wholly good; only it must be regretted that there is a good deal of narrowmindedness[24] and impatience among those who are actuated by it, not least in things that run counter to their credal beliefs. Another thing is the desire to oblige everybody to accept strict impositions laid upon them, without adequate reference to elements in human nature that are inconsistent with them and to intellectual disagreement.

It is strange that the good aspects of these three faculties in us tend to be contrary to each other. In their incompatibilities the good of each destroys the good of the other, and evil ensues, whereas their bad aspects confirm and serve each other in a mutual corroboration. The very virility of the vital force falls foul of reason and refuses to acknowledge its obligation to the latter or to be guided by its wisdom. And when the dictates or rules of conscience also oppose it, it takes no heed of them. Reason, on its part, has no will to recognise the force of what is instinctive in us, or to heed the directives and prohibitions of conscience; while the partisans of conscience think it good to stifle the vital force and to decry reason, lest it should detract from its authority. This conflict negates the good in these faculties of man. But when it comes to their evil results, the physical power, in full cry, joins forces with the delusions of the rational power and they conspire together with the bigotries and the restlessness of the religious outlook in its varied forms.

How can we attain a harmony between the features of these faculties in us that make for good, so that each might strengthen the other in a common welfare and our life be true and right? Each of these elements in the human make-up has its devotees and advocates, who hold the view that of itself alone it is adequate to life and that it can only fail if it is impeded and weakened by the others. The partisans of the first believe that instincts are invincible, that thwarting them provokes all kinds of psychological disorders and that any attempt to eliminate them is itself doomed to fail completely. They hold that the life of instinct conduces to conflict and the struggle to survive, which in turn leads to the survival of the fittest. Evil in this realm only arises when instincts are resisted and repressed. The advocates of reason want it to be paramount, ruling absolutely over the vital powers and controlling them as it will, ignoring meanwhile everything religious that does not agree with rational knowledge and experience. Reason, they hold, is sufficient for our guidance, if it is given sole authority over our affairs. It has only failed when overmastered by physical appetites, or when at other times conscience has hampered its course and dissipated its strength. The advocates of religion, too, wish to arrogate to their realm the whole of life, whether in things small or great, whether in what does or does not properly belong to creeds. They pay no attention to differences of temperament or of times. They have no will to accept anything from the realm of the instincts or of the mind that contravenes their preconceived ideas. Each group is set on the victory of that in which it believes, though this way of thinking is false. Such self-preoccupation is the source of trouble. Excessive growth of any of these factors in life increases their tyranny and intensifies the mutually obstructive character of their good features and the mutual stimulus of their evils. In any case, it is said, people differ in their susceptibility to the influence of each of them. They only profit from what they accept and then only are its good effects seen in them. But no! this is not the way to betterment. Each group going to fanatical extremes in its point of view offers no way of salvation. Nothing good will accrue from our laying down what people are to do with meticulous detail, asserting that he or she who adheres to these rules does well and he or she who contravenes them does wrong. Nor is there any benefit to be derived from the intensifying of one of these elements so that it lords over the others, however good it may be in itself. Even conscience, despite its potential benedictions, has never of itself alone accomplished the reform of humanity, save in the first periods of every religion, when religious expression was strong, when life was simple and people's minds docile. Then with the lengthening years conscience came to be estranged from life and reason, and when so enfeebled, people ceased to be moved by it: or else it grew more domineering, while reason paled and natural vigour dwindled. But the sole dominance of the vital instincts is an undoubted evil, which none will approve except those who are ignorant and barbarous, even though the partisans of this 'surrender to life' wax eloquent in praise of an order of things on that basis. As for reason, when it carries to excess its claim to authority – as is the case in our time – people find themselves in continual unease and constant fear on that account. We are today in the grip of the dominance of reason, with all its prestige, and we are awed by the potency for evil that is latent in its work. People nowadays are everlastingly talking about this evil and see a corresponding growth in the power of conscience and its latent benefits as absolutely necessary alongside the growth of science. But that is a rather empty sort of remark. If conscience, in the height of its vigour, was unable to prevent evil when reason was a feeble thing, it is still less qualified to prevent it when the evil has grown stronger.

Reason is constituted by its nature to direct. The nature of conscience is to restrain and warn. If each only adhered to its natural role the good effects of both would prevail. But to expect conscience to be a guide and reason a curb is to ask what is not within the nature of either.[25]

The true road to a sound welfare lies in the refining and defining of these elements of our constitution and in their being trained not to tyrannise over each other, even with a good intent. When good transgresses its proper limits it becomes evil, in that it throws things into imbalance. Only in moderation will these three be held together truly. The pulse of life will then be the matrix of activity, the rational faculty will guide, while conscience will act as a curb upon both, against extremes. Each will have its own wide field in which to function, a field which widens with the variety of human inclinations and aptitudes, and with the degree to which we are responsive to the good within us.

The majority of thinkers and reformers have taken the line that they should carefully delimit the ends in which the good and the right are constituted, together with the means to both. They have regarded all else as evil and false. But this is an illusion. It has not bettered the human condition at any time. It is rather our duty to define for people the range of evil and error and teach them that everything else is good and right, and that if they do not go wrong over the powers within them, they have deliverance from evil. To err over the true status of their physical life will mean lethargy or atrophy. To err over the true role of reason will mean ignorance. To go wrong over conscience is to fall a prey to idol worship – whatever the idols be – and to unbridled passion and human hatred. Let us teach them that they are otherwise free beings, as long as they shun these wrong attitudes. All else is good and right.

In the events of Good Friday all the factors in evil and sin were present. Every day of life its tragedy is repeated. Let men and women, therefore, take cognisance of what those factors are and eschew them. For thus they will come, to their joy and delight, upon a wide liberty in well doing, a liberty that makes of life a fine and gracious thing.

# Annexes

# Translator's Footnotes

1. Martin Buber, *Between Man and Man*, Routledge and Kegan Paul, London 1947, p. 109.

2. Walter de la Mare, 'Incomprehensible' from *Inward Companion*, p. 57, London 1950, quoted by permission of the Society of Authors, London.

3. This reference of the prosecutor to the possibility of being destroyed by thunder and lightning in Divine retribution or visitation is a recurrent theme. The mufti roundly reproaches the prosecutor for these sentiments (p. 54) and returns to the topic in his remarks in the hall of meeting (p. 82). The learned doctor, the merchant's friend, suggests a similar idea (p. 63). It figures again (p. 199) in the discussion under the shadow of the Cross between the Wise Man and the Athenian philosopher. It is a clear echo of Surah ii. 19, where unbelievers, overtaken in a violent storm, put their fingers in their ears for fear of death from thunderbolt or lightning flash. But here, by a strange reversal, what unbelievers guiltily fear is turned into an obviously improper argument on the lips of reputable custodians of religion. This would seem to be part of the author's underlying thesis that orthodoxy and unbelief may have much in common when it comes to resisting the dictates of conscience where these counter what is either familiar or convenient.

4. The reference is to Surah xii, the Chapter in the Qur'án which deals at length with the Joseph narrative. Here Joseph does not, as in the Genesis story, personally interpret to Pharaoh the latter's dreams about the ears of corn and the cattle. The liberated

prisoner, who for long years had forgotten Joseph, goes to the prison at Pharaoh's behest and brings back verbally Joseph's interpretation of the dreams. Only then does Pharaoh command Joseph to be brought in and the latter seizes the occasion to secure first his vindication from the calumnies of the women who had maligned him. Thus Pharaoh's exaltation of Joseph to high honour in the land turns solely on the verbal interpretation, brought by another, and on a belated admission of Joseph's innocence.

5. The phrase 'manifest error' is a very familiar Quranic one. (Surah iii. 164; vi. 74. vii. 60 and some thirty or more other passages). It refers to the state of unbelief and idolatry preceding Islam and to the obduracy with which the light of truth is resisted as, for example, by the contemporaries of Abraham. The mufti here extends the phrase to cover the vagaries and obtusenesses of men of the true faith and even of the very custodians of orthodoxy. It is a healthily novel idea for 'men of religion' to be found in 'manifest error.'

6. The fact that God does not guide those for whom He wills perverseness, that, indeed, there is no guide for them, is a familiar note in Quranic teaching (cf. Surah vii. 186 et al.) The ultimate meaning is that people, by their irresponsiveness to truth, grow steadily more inured against it, whereas attitudes of obedience and recognition of truth ripen and mature into increasing knowledge. Thus there is a constant association in the Qur'án between 'signs' and the attentive mind and submissive will. The Qur'án itself, with all its verses (these latter being called *Ayát* or 'signs') is the supreme token of God's communicativeness. But there are numerous 'signs' of God's will and power in nature and in man's heart. (cf. Surah xli. 43: 'We show them our signs in all the realms of the earth and in the very souls of men.') But these 'signs' are always to and for 'a people with their wits about them' – *illá Qaumin Ya'qilún*. Only those who are ready to hearken and ponder (as in the case of the New Testament parables) are illuminated. The casual and the flippant, or the prejudiced, are thereby incapacitated from recognition as

long as they maintain these attitudes. Truth exacts its own proper conditions of attentiveness, foregoing of prejudice and readiness for obedience. Always there is this reciprocity between sign and meaning, between truth in availability and truth in apprehension, between being and knowledge. True belief is a kinship of the soul with truth. It may be conjectured that the essential significance of the 'sign' in Islam underlies the author's exploration of the import 'signified' in Good Friday.

Aspects of 'signs' and their recognition concern us later in several other contexts (cf. p. 114, and see note 22).

7. The Arabic phrase rendered 'the Lord Christ' presents somewhat of a problem of translation. The author it will be noted refers mostly to Jesus under the phrases 'the teacher of the new gospel,' 'the innovator of the new heresy,' 'the master,' 'the rabbi' etc. The name Jesus does not occur, nor does 'Isá, which is its Quranic counterpart. The Qur'án, however, in several places uses the title 'Christ,' the Messiah, usually with the phrase 'son of Mary.' In popular Muslim usage the word Sayyid, or Lord, almost invariably prefaces any mention of Christ, as a token of veneration and honour. The same word is also used of the Prophet Muhammad and in either case may have the possessive pronoun 'our.' Because of the deference it expresses it seems right that it should here be capitalised, though Christian readers will realise that the usage 'Lord' implies no Divine status nor any recognition of Christian understandings of the Lord. It is for this other reason that nouns relating to Jesus in this book except 'Lord' are not in translation capitalised, since for western readers capitalising might imply something other than the Muslim connotation of the words. The Arabic language of course neatly escapes the dilemma by capitalising nothing. The phrase 'the Lord Christ' occurs also on pp. 106, 111 (where Mary speaks), 114, 120, 192, 200 and 202.

8. Caiaphas' dubiety about 'weakness' ever being one of the attributes of God outside Jesus' teaching has rather a Muslim ring. There is an echo of it on p. 63 where it is argued that God is not

so weak as to need a sign to convince people that a servant of His is being wronged. The assumption is that He will directly intervene to save him, as a more appropriately efficient and Divine proceeding. The same instinct, metaphysically seen, underlies the whole Muslim concept of the Divine rescue of the Christ from the Cross, since Divine purposes cannot readily, or properly, be conceived of as making their way through a crisis of apparent defeat. It is precisely in such weakness that, as the Christian sees it, an enterprise, Divinely conceived as reconciling and forgiving, must necessarily make its way.

9. This warning against hyperbole in language may well have arisen from considerations about Arabic of which modern Arab writers have been conscious. Cf. Ahmad Amín in *Faid al-Khátir* (Cairo, 1938–50). Note also the Wise Man's misgiving about fine words on p. 210.

10. The actual phrase used here of Christ is an echo of the traditional devotional words *La Haulah wa la Quwwah illá ilaihi* 'There is no might nor power save His' used in ascription of praise to God in Muslim liturgies.

11. The words rendered 'oblivious in oblivion' belong to Surah xix. 23 where Mary the Virgin in the pains of travail seeks shelter under a palm tree and cries out: 'Would that I had died and become oblivious in oblivion.'

12. Deep contemporary questions in the Muslim world attach to this issue of the nature of the relevance the documentary revelation has to the details of daily life and social institutions (see also p. 184). A Report in 1956 of a Government Commission in Pakistan on Marriage and Family Laws well illustrates what is at issue in the evolution of the Roman soldier's ideas. The majority opinion in the Report declares: 'So far as the Holy Book is concerned the laws and injunctions promulgated therein deal mostly with basic principles and vital problems and consist of

answers to the questions which arose while the Holy Book was being revealed . . . As nobody can comprehend the infinite variety of human relations for all time, occasions and epochs, the Prophet of Islam left a large sphere free for legislative enactments and judicial decisions.' (*Gazette of Pakistan*, June 20th 1956, p. 1199). One minority member, however, scornfully disputed this notion by asking whether one could revise the Qur'án so that it read: '"This day I have perfected unto your religion," only of course it will need making right by Commissions and Committees,' a violent disclaimer that begs the question but certainly measures the depth and range of the whole controversy between literalism and spiritual loyalty (see *Gazette of Pakistan*, August 30th 1956, p. 1563).

13. The 'I' which opens this paragraph is intriguing. For it is obviously the medical author speaking, not one of the anguished watchers beside the sick girl. Similarly on p. 190 the author permits himself an observation based no doubt on professional interest and even allows himself the precise reference to the days of the Second World War.

14. The prophecy is true enough, for the meaning of our Lord's remark, as recorded in S. John ii. 4, has been frequently discussed in Muslim writing on the New Testament. Some within the Ahmadiyyah Movements have considered it a discourteous remark which either suggests the unreliability of the narrative or (if accepted) the incivility of Jesus. The Muslim is prompted by the Qur'án to hold Mary in deep veneration, and this makes the perplexity all the greater and the readier. All things considered, it is a perplexity that need not be so acute, if due attention is paid to the inoffensive significance of the remark in the original (in which 'woman' has nothing of its contemporary English connotation) and to the sequel of the narrative itself where Mary herself evidently took her Son's words as prefacing a full meeting of her wishes.

15. This leading question and all that underlies the subsequent discussion (and the discourse of the Wise Man on p. 131) are

central to the early history of Islam which followed the Quranic dictum that 'war is better than *Fitnah*' (See Introduction and cf. Surah ii. 191, quoted on p. 124, and Surah ii. 217). It is part of the author's insistence on the commonness of moral problems and of human temptations that he is able to broach an issue central to Islam's origins in terms of a perplexity agonising Christ's disciples.

16. The ultimate source of the characteristically Christian sense of sin is perhaps the biggest single issue, theologically, of *Qaryah Zálimah*. As suggested in the Introduction, it is the translator's belief that it springs from that contemplation of the human scene and situation, as these are epitomised in the events and antecedents of Good Friday, with all their stark revelation of human waywardness and the reach of sin and pride into all our judgements and choices, both personal and collective. Though he has movingly portrayed and pondered this disclosure of humanity and evil, the author has a different interpretation in his analysis of Christian instinctive attitudes. All readers will be grateful for the clear and illuminating outline, printed here in the Appendix, which Dr. Hussein has contributed in his kindly answer to enquiry on this basic point.

It may be added that there is a refrain in the Qur'án, not frequent but yet haunting, on this theme of 'failure'. It hinges on the verb *farrata*, with its derivatives. Surah vi. 31 pictures the unbelievers on the day of judgement confessing that they have neglected much during their lives, that they have left things undone. By contrast (verse 38 of the same Surah) God has in no way failed in His Book, there is no omission in His revelatory work and the varieties of living communities, beasts that prowl and birds that fly, all have their ordered ways. Angels, too, (Surah vi. 61) do not fail or turn negligent in their guardianship of souls beyond the grave. Surah xii. 80 has the eldest of Jacob's sons reminding his brethren, in their extremity over Benjamin's predicament, that they had 'failed in their faith' towards Joseph years before. Surah xxxix. 56 imagines the despairing soul at judgement confessing how it deplores its utter neglect of God in life. In every case the word used is that employed here to describe this dereliction of duty, this incriminating sense of omission and demise of fidelity on the part of the disciples.

17. Again a phrase quoted from the Qur'án, used in a sense that is evidently deplorable and set on the lips of a speaker who is plainly in the wrong, whereas its original sense is praiseworthy and its source exemplary. Surah xxiii. 66 has 'We (God) shall say: Many a time were my revelations recited to you but you turned back upon your heels.' Evidently the devil can quote Scripture for his purpose in more traditions than one. Certainly the invocation of a phrase of Holy Writ is no guarantee of validity in the argument that invokes it. It is interesting that the orator begins with a famous supposed remark of Admiral Nelson and ends with the Qur'án: he opens with Trafalgar and concludes at Mecca.

18. There is something of a play on words in the original here which is somewhat feebly essayed in the English: 'when matters drive us we derive.'

19. Here in pleading his will to conform resignedly to Rome's outlook and to Roman ways, Pilate uses the term *Ijmá'*, or consensus, which has its technical sense in the Islamic system where such common mind is one of the sources or roots of law. (See the Introduction). The whole point of it is that the communal, the collective, the corporate and general, preserves and directs the individual and private. Heresy is individualism. The author's great problem, however, is to discover a means whereby the moral sensitivity of the individual can assert itself in and over the community. It is significant that when Pilate despairs of 'truth' he falls back upon the collective.

20. 'Lawless movement' here renders the crucial word *Fitnah* on which comment was made in the Introduction. See also note 15. It contains within itself the twin ideas of dissension and sedition. Surah ix. 48 speaks of the waverers who were disinclined to go forth to battle and thereby 'created dissension' in the ranks.

Likewise in Surah iii. 7 tendentious exegesis which fixes on 'ambiguous' or uncategorical passages of the Qur'án is said to create dissension and discord. Elsewhere it is the kindred thought of hostility to the established order or doctrine which is in mind. Surah viii. 39 reads: 'Fight them (the detractors) until resistance (*Fitnah* – sedition, counter-doctrine, or obduracy) is no more.' Such resistance presents a mortal threat to the system it defies. So Surah lx. 5 reads: 'Do not expose us to the conspiracy (*Fitnah*) of the unbelievers' with the implication that otherwise we will become a prey to them. It is clear, then, how *Fitnah* comes to have the sense of mortal trial, 'existential temptation' so to speak, as in Surah xvii. 60, ix. 49 and viii. 25. The connotations of the word plainly suit the crisis implicit for Jewry in the mission and message of Jesus. (Attention may be drawn to reflections on the meaning of *Fitnah* in *The Muslim World*, Vol. xlviii. No. 1, Jan. 1958, pp. 1–5).

21. Here the philosopher regards the Wise Man's view as having more to it than the shepherdess's. On p. 195 he declares that he finds it hard to choose between their respective ideas. They are equally puerile. In answer to the desire for elucidation on this apparent inconsistency the author says: 'The opinions of the Wise Man and the shepherdess are both one-sided and are foolish only to those who know better and more. But how much more is needed to make the opinion decidedly not foolish. The point of the passage is that every one is foolish to those who are higher and are thus in a position to know better. Who can decide that a certain opinion is so high that there is no higher one to which the former would look foolish?'

22. Again the author insists on the affinity between the sign and the perceptive soul – a thought that underlies the perpetual Quranic link between the 'signs' in which God speaks and the attentive, receptive, imaginative heart. For a sign is not truly a sign save in and as its significance is realised. It is the place or point of a transaction: it is meaning in mediation and only where there is apprehension has there been communication. The same underlying

truth belongs to the realm of the Biblical parables and the Christian sacraments.

It is perhaps worthy of note that the only person who comes to a different mind at the Cross, from that which characterised him before, is the Jewish leader.

23. It is a characteristic feature of the Islamic ethical concept that God makes His normal demands feasible and 'convenient' to human nature. The fast of Ramadan, for example, lasts a month, to enjoin and train the soul's supremacy over the body. But it has its term, for the good things of life are meant to be enjoyed and asceticism is no end in itself (cf. Surah ii. 185 on those who are exempted from the fast either totally or temporarily) This point of Islam's feasibility to and for the natural person has figured conspicuously in Muslim discussion of Christianity, whose ethical scheme is said to be lofty but impracticable, noble but unrealistic. The Christian, rather, sees the lightness of God's demands (cf. St. Matthew xi. 30) not in their approximation to his own unaided capacities, but to the enabling, indwelling of the Divine Love, re-creating men and women and thus giving them a new dimension of ethical feasibility and of redeemed being.

24. 'Narrowmindedness' here is the English of a frequent Quranic thought, lit. 'constriction of the bosom.' Surah xciv. 1 speaks of God asking Muhammad, rhetorically: 'Did we not enlarge for thee thy bosom?' and Moses prays in Surah xx. 26 that God would enlarge his breast as a condition, so comments the great Al-Baidáwí, of his adequately assuming the tasks about to be laid on him. Surah xxxix. 22 refers to him 'whose heart is enlarged unto surrender.' This largeness or hospitality of heart to truth and vocation is contrasted with narrow-heartedness, which is a state of rejection of light and refusal of response (See Surah vi. 126).

25. The reader who has formed the general impression that *Qaryah Zálimah* holds conscience to be the only valid guide may be nonplussed by this remark that it is improper to expect guidance

from conscience. The author has commented extensively as follows on his meaning here: 'Conscience is the *leitmotif* of the whole book. It does not fit exactly into what theologians, philosophers or moralists mean by conscience. To some a mere postulate, to others it means simply all that is good in us, to others a conception which I deliberately kept vague for convenience. It becomes therefore a matter of importance to define exactly what I mean by it.

To me conscience is a law as certain and as demonstrable as the law of gravity or the laws of biology, with the difference inherent in the material on which these laws act. It is natural because it is an extension into the human psychic field of a law which is universal in all living creatures and which has been demonstrated beyond doubt in physiology, i.e. the law of inhibition. As the essential character of moral laws is inhibitory, and as inhibition is widespread in nature, there is every reason to believe that it exists in the human psyche in the form of conscience.

'It is also the highest law known to us. To explain this superiority I have to call in a theory which I hold about the laws of nature and which I call the hierarchy of laws. Kant in one of his most celebrated passages stresses that when he considers the moral law within him he feels that he is greater than the firmament and the stars. But he never explained why the moral law should have that superiority over all else in nature. The theory of the hierarchy of laws offers a scientific proof of that fact.

'A law is superior to another when it can only act on things already acted upon by the latter. Thus chemical laws are superior to nuclear ones, physical laws are superior to chemical, biological are superior to material. At the same time, and as a corollary to this rule, the higher laws act on more complex things.

'We are, therefore, superior to animals. For the laws of intelligence and reason only act on organisms already subject to biological laws of animals. As it is only on intelligent and reasonable people that moral laws can act, these are obviously superior to the laws of intelligence and reason. It is irrelevant how great intelligence or reason happen to be. The moral laws are always superior to them, just as the bee is superior to an oak tree, because its laws are higher and more complex. Thus the simplest person who has faith and morals is superior to the most intelligent and reasonable person who does not admit moral laws.

'It is not possible here to develop this theory in all its implications. I would like, however, to stress that conscience is mainly prohibitive (hence its imperative character) and that it is natural and also the highest law of which we are cognisant.'

Thus, in relation to the immediate point with which this note began he adds: 'Although it is possible to be positively guided by conscience, the main power of conscience being inhibitive and prohibitive, it is mainly a guide to us in avoiding wrong. When it acts excessively it can have a paralysing effect. The correct balance between the forces acting on us is the only assurance of a proper state of perfection and bliss.'

Dr. Hussein deals with this subject in a forthcoming book *The Unity of Knowledge (Wihdat-al Ma'rifah)*. The translator is deeply grateful to him for his kindness and help in elucidating these and other points. In a final comment on the question of what happened at the cross he adds: 'The idea of a substitute for Christ is a very crude way of explaining the Quranic text. They had to explain a lot to the masses. No cultured Muslim believes in this nowadays. The text is taken to mean that the Jews thought they killed Christ but God raised him unto Him in a way we can leave unexplained among the several mysteries which we have taken for granted on faith alone.'

# Author's Note:
# The Apostles' Self-Reproach

The idea must have occurred to me on reading Freud's book *Moses and Monotheism*. It is a book which shows all the audacity and ingenuity of the author as a researcher, but lacks the close-knit argumentation of his earlier works — a quality one appreciates in Freud even when one disagrees with him on all points.

In this book he suggests that nations, races, religious and cultured groups can be the subject of psychological complexes (in the best meaning of the word), very similar to those of individuals. Starting from this postulate I began to investigate the possibility of the existence of such complexes. The first object of my study was the Jews. It occurred to me that the crucial event which shaped the psychological structure of the Jews was the Exodus. It was a major psychical stress (or trauma) occurring in the infancy of the race and it left an indelible mark on their mentality, very much in the way that events in infancy influence the mentality of people as they grow up. Some unbelievers would deny the whole historical event but this is immaterial to our argument. For even if the Exodus is only a legend, it is remarkably expressive, in a most poetical manner, which can only be described as Divine[1], of the essence of a race's mentality unequalled in the history of legends. The relation between the Exodus and fundamental Jewish psychology would still exist.

What is the essence of the Exodus? It is essentially the escape of the Jews from certain and utter annihilation by a most extraordinary miracle. Thus abject despair and unbounded hope exist simultaneously in the mind of the Jews. They live as if they were at one and the same time on the brink of total destruction and on the eve of the most resounding victory, and they act accordingly! Had they been exposed to a less certain danger and had they fought, even unsuccessfully, for their own defence and had they been saved by a less remarkable miracle, the effect on their psychological structure would have been less.

In seeking for a similarly crucial event in the history of Christianity, I considered that the failure of the Apostles on the day of Crucifixion to strike a single blow (with the exception of the earlier abortive attempt by St. Peter) to save their Master must have left an indelible mark on their psychical structure. This would not be entirely removed by the fact that they were obeying superior orders. For these orders remained to them an unexplained enigma at least for some time.

I contend that the Apostles on that day had no idea of the Divine significance of Crucifixion or that it had been decreed from eternity. They had no idea of Redemption, Atonement or the role of Jesus Christ as Saviour. All this (I hope I am not wrong here) was defined and explained clearly by the most remarkable of men, St. Paul. On the day of Crucifixion the Apostles were mere men, leaving their Master to be tortured and crucified by His enemies. Even in obedience this must have been most distressing to them. The obvious conclusion would be that even the best of people are, on great occasions, too blind to see their way to right unless they are guided by a superior hand. Such a psychological stress could not be without effect on their psyche. Is it not just possible that such effects can be inherited? The best Christian in his or her most sublime moments is a sad person.

I believe that the corresponding crucial event in the history of Islam, which affected the mentality of Muslims in a similar manner, was the little skirmish of Badr, where three hundred odd Muslims, who thus far had no social or political standing whatsoever, met a thousand of the bravest and most celebrated men of Quraish and routed them. On that day Islam came into the open and developed high-handedly with a good deal of pride. Had the Muslims let their Prophet die at the hands of Quraish without striking a blow for his safety, the history of Islam would probably have been identical with the history of Christianity, growing through submission, humility and heroic resistance to persecution.

The sense of guilt and self-reproach the Apostles felt on the day of Crucifixion has, thus, no relation to the Divine drama which happened under their very eyes and which they did not fully understand. But, as mere men, they must have reproached themselves for what they failed to do.

1. See an Essay: 'The Best of Stories' in my *Mutanawwi'át*, Cairo, 2nd edition, 'Miscellaneous Themes' pp. 27–38, which deals at length with the history of the Exodus. Translated in *The Muslim World*, Vol xlix, No. i, Jan. 1959.